The Business of Writing

ELIZABETH DUCIE

To Michael as ever; without you, there would have been no Heathside and, therefore, no book.

Contents

List of Figures

List of Abbreviations

ALCS	Authors' Licensing and Collecting Society
ALLi	Alliance of Independent Authors
DBA	Doing Business As
EIN	Employer Identification Number
EU	European Union
GDPR	General Data Protection Regulation
HMRC	Her Majesty's Revenue and Customs
IRS	Internal Revenue Services
ISBN	International Standard Book Number
MBA	Masters in Business Administration
N/A	Not Applicable
NFIB	National Federation of Independent Business
NZ	New Zealand
PAYE	Pay As You Earn
PDR	Plan, Do and Review
P&L	Profit and Loss
PLR	Public Lending Rights
RNA	Romantic Novelists Association

SBA	Small Business Administration
SMART	Specific, Measurable, Achievable, Relevant, Time-related
SWWJ	Society of Women Writers and Journalists
U3A	University of the Third Age
UK	United Kingdom of Great Britain and N. Ireland
USA	United States of America
VAT	Value Added Tax
VAT MOSS	VAT Mini One Stop Shop
WI	Women's Institute
Womags	Women's Magazines

Introduction

I've been writing technically for most of my working life. I've been writing creatively since 2005 and I've been working as a full-time writer since 2012.

However, I am also a small business owner—and have been since 1992. In the first year of our operation, we made more profit than a well-known computer manufacturer. (OK, so that was the year that company made a loss—but you must admit it sounds impressive!) I've taught myself, through trial and error, to set up and run systems that work. Occasionally, I use the services of other individuals or organisations. In fact, knowing when to use a professional approach rather than DIY is an important skill in running a small business. But mostly I've done it myself.

I studied Business Administration at Cranfield School of Management and graduated with an MBA. I'm a scientist by education and training. I enjoy maths, project planning and system management. But most writers I meet are the complete opposite. They are horrified at the thought of having to stop creating to do the paperwork, the administration, and the 'boring bits' of running a business.

The Business of Writing is a toolbox of business skills for writers. My aim is to provide a simple route by which you can set up and run your own small businesses. I want to identify the 'basic minimum standards' that must be achieved, while freeing you to spend the maximum possible time doing what you really want to—writing.

I am neither an accountant nor a lawyer. I am simply a business owner with more than twenty-five years' experience. There will be times when taking the advice of another business practitioner is not enough.

At those times, you need to consult the appropriate professional. I will keep reminding you of that throughout the book.

Although I've worked all over the world and seen a variety of business systems in operation, my own business is based in the United Kingdom. Hence, inevitably, my knowledge of business systems tends to be biased towards there. The first edition of this book was very much UK-focused. This second edition has been expanded to bring in a wider focus, particularly the United States.

Throughout the book, I will be identifying the questions you need to ask, rather than providing the answers (since they will often vary with individual circumstances). This book is therefore intended to be useful to all writers who are small business owners, wherever they may be located.

The material in this book is taken from the lectures I have presented in recent years, and from associated blog posts. It was originally published as a series of three ebooks—and these are still available for purchase individually, if you are only interested in one part of the process.

I don't claim to have invented any of the tools and techniques we are going to discuss. I have never believed in re-inventing the wheel; in fact I am a firm believer in the CASE approach: Copy And Steal Everything. Having said that, I always ask for permission before quoting someone else's work and I always give credit where it's due. So I guess it's more Copy And Borrow Everything, but CABE isn't such an effective acronym.

As they used to say on *Who Wants to be a Millionaire,* the questions are only easy if you know the answers. There are a lot of writers out there for whom a toolbox of business skills is completely new and so the questions are not easy. This book is written for you.

Section 1: Business Start-Up

1. Business Planning

1.1 Introduction

The starting point for every new business should be a good, clear business plan—and your writing business is no different. It's an important tool, for example, in talking to potential financial backers, whether that's the friendly local bank-manager (and I bet there are some of those out there, somewhere) or Great-aunt Lucy, who's loaded and looking for a safe investment for her cash. But more importantly, it's a great way of organising your thoughts and plans into a logical framework. And that's critical, for example, if you're planning on taking that huge step of ditching the day job and making writing your full-time business.

A business plan shouldn't be a complicated document to develop. Essentially, it's a road map and therefore can be a great planning tool at the beginning. You probably won't have to look at it too often once you get started and know where you're going. But, it can also be useful to revisit it every year to see whether your predictions were correct and to check whether your objectives are still the same as before or whether you need to change direction.

Of course, not everyone who writes a business plan is just starting out. There will be some of you who've been working for yourself for a while; maybe even for a long time. And maybe you feel you've lost your way. Or you want to take it to the next level. Possibly move from writing in your spare time, or part time, to full time. In that case, preparing a business plan is a good way of clarifying the steps you need to take to make the next move. But I would suggest you clear your mind of what you've been doing so far and try to think as though you're just starting out. That way, you're less likely to fall foul of assumptions that might not be valid ones. For example, the editorial policies of magazines have been known to change overnight. Your previous experience with submission and acceptance of short stories might not necessarily be valid going forward.

Preparing a business plan is a simple process that can be done easily in a short space of time. It's something you should be able to do in your lunch hour (or at most, a week's worth of lunch hours) by thinking about a series of questions. In fact, it's those questions and the responses you come up with, that are more important than the actual format of the plan itself. So, here are my suggestions for the questions you need to ask yourself before writing that first business plan.

1.2 What do I/could I write?

In other words, what are you going to sell to people? It may be fiction: short stories, novellas or novels. It may be non-fiction: articles for magazines, newspapers, websites; textbooks or how-to books on your specialist subject; memoir, biography or autobiography. You might prefer to try your hand at ghost writing, which could be fiction or non-fiction. Starting out, it's likely to be a mix of the above and it may well always be a wide range. You need to start with a clear idea of the type of writing you are going to offer.

1.3 What writerly services could I sell?

Few writers make a living from writing alone, certainly in the early stages. This is particularly true for anyone wishing to write fiction. Are there any other activities connected with writing that you could offer? Are there subjects, connected either with your writing or other aspects of your life, which you could convert into talks for organisations such as the Women's Institute (WI), the University of the Third Age (U3A) or your own industry associations? Speaking engagements often have a double benefit. As well as the fee, there is the opportunity to sell your books, either at the time or later, online. We'll come back to this topic in the chapter on Reaching The

Customer. Or are there aspects of your writing you could convert into a training course or workshop?

1.4 Who will buy my writing/services?

Who are the people who need your writing? Are you selling to other writing businesses: editors or publishers of books or magazines? Or maybe you will be selling to non-writing businesses: whether that's a large corporation which needs your expertise in writing technical reviews or copy for their annual report; or the guy down the road who needs help writing the copy for his new website? Alternatively, are you planning to sell direct to your readership via independent publishing?

If you are offering talks or putting on courses, will you do it as a freelancer, or via an organisation? The former is more cost effective, as you keep all the fees yourself, but on the other hand, you'll need to devote more time to organising the event in the first place, plus identifying appropriate potential clients and getting in touch with them. It's a question of balance.

1.5 How will I promote my writing?

This is critical. If you don't promote your writing, no-one will know about it and you will have no customers. And, of course, the answer to this question is linked to the previous one. Once you know who your customers are and where to find them, you can plan your promotion. This can be as simple as word-of-mouth networking or as complex as a full marketing campaign with paid advertisements and giveaways.

These days, your promotion will almost certainly contain a large element of social networking. So if you're someone who sniffs at the thought of using Facebook or Twitter; or refuses to even learn what Pinterest or Instagram are; I'm afraid you're going to have to get over it! Without an online presence, you will be invisible. But don't despair. There's plenty of training out there in the form of blogs, webinars, YouTube videos etc. And who knows, once you dive in, you might find you quite enjoy it.

1.6 What should I charge for my writing?

You need a clear view of the appropriate price for your writing. If it's too high, people won't be willing to pay. If it's too low, they may be suspicious of the quality and go elsewhere. Have a look at what the competition is doing and decide on the right level to pitch it at. But remember, customers will often expect to pay less for an untested product, so you may have to be willing to compromise at first, until you have a proven track record. We'll look at this in a bit more detail in the chapter on Thinking About Finances.

1.7 What are the financial implications?

Once you have a clear view of what you're going to sell, to whom, how and at what price, you can then do the sums and see whether it's going to work or not; whether your plans are financially viable.

Make a sensible estimate of expected sales, sometimes called a budget, over the first year, remembering it might be slow to start with. It's better to be pessimistic at this point. If you underestimate, it's not a problem. If you overestimate, you could get into difficulties. Then determine the costs you need to incur to support that level of sales. Remember to consider direct costs like materials (although for a writer, these are relatively low, unless you have 'shiny notebook syndrome') plus indirect costs like electricity, postage and internet charges. Compare money coming in with money going out. Is there likely to be a surplus or will you need to make up a shortfall to start with? If the latter is more likely, identify sources of finance, whether it's selling the car, borrowing from friends or relatives, applying for grants, or going to the bank for a loan, although I certainly wouldn't recommend this latter route for a new writer. We will return to this discussion later in the chapter on Thinking About Finances.

1.8 What format for my plan?

As with so many questions we're going to ask throughout this series of books, the answer is not straightforward and will depend on your personal circumstances. A business plan being used by an individual to get their ideas sorted in their head will be a much simpler document than one being prepared as part of a submission for a grant or other support. From page 18 onward, you'll find some worked examples using a couple of simple templates. In the reference section you'll find details of more complex forms provided by both public bodies and private organisations. Take your pick. But as always, I would advise going for the simplest format that suits your purpose. There really is no need to complicate life more than necessary.

1.9 Meet Anthea Rosewood

Setting up your own small business can be a daunting experience. I should know. I've done it more than once over the past twenty-five years. So, I'm not going to ask you to do it on your own. Meet Anthea Rosewood, a full-time librarian living in the Southwest of England. We'll be accompanying Anthea on her journey throughout this book and she'll be setting you an example which you can follow, or learn from, if you wish.

Anthea has a degree in English and a Masters in Creative Writing, which she's completed via a distance learning course over the past two years. She's been writing in her spare time for more than ten years and has had some success with competitions. She's also had many short stories published by *People's Friend* and *Woman's Weekly*, so she has a track record and is not an unknown. However, her ambition is to become a full-time writer and, at some point, a novelist. She's been given the opportunity to reduce her librarian role to three days per week and she's investigating the possibility of taking the first step towards achieving her ambition.

1.10 Conclusion

Preparing a business plan is a straightforward process that can be done relatively easily in a short space of time, such as over lunch. However, it's an important first step in getting your business started. It could be the most important lunch hour of your life.

The purpose of this book is to provide you with a simple process for getting your business set up. You will find from page 18 onward some simple templates I've prepared for you. The plan can be written on a couple of sheets of paper, as a series of paragraphs, as a list of bullet points, as a mind map or however you wish. There are no right answers in all this; and it's your plan, after all. However, what you produce should be feasible and a realistic prediction of what you can do, rather than an unachievable wish-list.

If you wish to develop something more complex, the reference section includes links to other templates and sources of advice.

1.11 Worked Examples

Anthea Rosewood has developed her business plan using two different approaches. On page 18, you can see it in traditional format. On page 28 she has also used a variation on the business model canvas.

Figure 1 Business Plan (Traditional)

Business Plan (Traditional)

Owner: Anthea Rosewood

Business name: Anthea Rosewood Writes

Business address: Honeysuckle Cottage, Fieldfare Road, Moortown, Devon

Business website: www.anthearosewood.co.uk

Date: 1st January 2018

Executive Summary

The Business: I intend to establish a business as a writer and provider of writerly services.
Products: In the first three years, my writing will consist of short stories sold to magazines and entered in competitions; plus letters and short pieces sold to magazines. In addition, I will give talks to local membership groups. I will also run workshops and short courses on creative writing for beginners.
Customers: For the writing, I have an established client list; but will be expanding this over time. My talks will be to WI, U3A, Probus and other local groups. My workshops and courses will be to beginner writers.
The Future: My long-term aim is to become a full-time writer of both fiction and non-fiction. The first three years of the business will serve as an opportunity to establish a secure income stream; to raise my profile as a writer; to explore the possibility of seeking a commission for a non-fiction book; and to begin my journey towards writing a series of steampunk Victorian novels.

Products/Services

Product description: Short stories for women's magazines

Already selling? Y	If no, when will it go on sale? N/A

Target audience: the following are examples only o Womags in UK: People's Friend; Woman's Weekly; My Weekly; Take A Break o Womags in USA: The Sun Magazine; The Threepenny Review o Womags in Australia: The Australian Women's Weekly; Quadrant; Woman's Day o Womags in Canada: Descant; The Fiddlehead; The Malahat Review; Queen's Quarterly o Womags in NZ: Freelance; New Zealand Woman's Day; Takahe

Distribution channels: o UK: Via post or email, depending on requirements of the individual magazine o Overseas: online submissions only

Direct costs: Postage, paper and envelopes where magazines require hard copy submissions (UK only). £1 per submission. Copies of magazines for research purposes. £5 per month.

Price: Varies between £80 and £200 per story sold. Assume an average of £150.

Profit margin: 98% in UK; 100% overseas per story sold.

Estimated sales: 6 stories per month submitted with a success rate of 50%; £450 per month Plus annual payment from ALCS of £150.

Product description: Short stories for competitions	
Already selling? Y	If no, when will it go on sale? N/A
Target audience: Any suitable competition which accepts online submissions; prose only; stories for adults only.	
Distribution channels: online submissions only.	
Direct costs: Entry fees for each competition. Assume an average of £5.	
Price: Prizes vary between £100 and £500. Assume an average of £250.	
Profit margin: 98% per competition win.	
Estimated sales: 50 stories per year entered with a success rate of 10%; £1250 per year.	

Product description: Letters and short pieces to magazines	
Already selling? N	If no, when will it go on sale? April 2018
Target audience: UK women's magazines as per short story submissions.	
Distribution channels: Via post or email, depending on requirements of the individual magazine	
Direct costs: Postage, paper and envelopes where magazines require hard copy submissions (UK only). £1 per submission.	
Price: Varies between small payment and other compensation such as garden centre vouchers. Assume average of £25.	
Profit margin: 96% per piece published	

Estimated sales: 10 pieces per month submitted with a success rate of 10%. £25 per month.

Product description: Talks to WI, U3A, Probus and similar groups on life as a country librarian; or writing short stories for magazines and competitions.	
Already selling? N	If no, when will it go on sale? April 2018
Target audience: WI, U3A, Probus and similar groups located within 20 miles drive of home. Where a longer journey is required, this will be considered, but additional mileage will be charged.	
Distribution channels: Face-to-face at groups' regular meeting places.	
Direct costs: Mileage charged at 45p per mile; maximum of £18 per return journey.	
Price: £50 including travel expenses.	
Profit margin: Maximum of £32 per talk.	
Estimated sales: 1 talk per month from January 2019 onwards. Groups book speakers up to a year in advance.	

Product description: Beginners' Creative Writing workshops (one-off 2-hour session) and courses (ten weekly 2-hour sessions).	
Already selling? N	If no, when will it go on sale? April 2018
Target audience: New writers who want to learn how to write short stories for magazines or competitions. In groups of between 6 and 10.	
Distribution channels: Face-to-face in a local venue.	

Direct costs: Venue hire £10 per hour. Preparation of materials: £10.
Price: £10 per session per person. £60 to £100 income per session.
Profit margin: £30 to £70 per session, depending on number of delegates. Assume an average of 8 delegates (£50)
Estimated sales: One workshop per month April to August 2018; one workshop and one short course per quarter from September 2018.

Marketing Strategy: General

- Website and weekly blog about all things writerly.
- Guest posts on other bogs.
- Social media to drive people to my blog: Facebook, Twitter (#Mondayblogs; #wwwblogs).
- Social media to interact with other writers: Facebook groups such as Book Connectors, Southwest Authors and Writers, West of England Authors, Womag Writers and Company, The People's Friend. Twitter groups such as Devon Book Hour.
- Email list for regular newsletters and one-off announcements.
- Local radio appearances: Mainstream local radio stations such as BBC Radio Devon, BBC Radio Cornwall; community radio stations such as Tiverton Community Radio, Riviera FM, Phoenix FM.

- Videos: via YouTube channel, publicised via social media.
- Talks at local libraries.

Marketing Strategy: Specific

Product: Short stories for women's magazines; Short stories for competitions; Letters and short pieces to magazines.

No specific marketing required in advance since submissions are made against calls and decisions made by reading/judging panels.

Any successes can be leveraged in press releases as part of the general marketing; also building the CV in preparation for submissions to agents/editors in the future.

Product: Talks to WI, U3A, Probus and similar groups on life as a country librarian; or writing short stories for magazines and competitions.

- Audition for WI speakers' book.
- Use group websites and personal contacts to make direct contact with programme secretaries.
- Use networking groups to request recommendations.
- Request recommendations following all successful talks.

Product: Beginners' Creative Writing workshops (one-off 2-hour session) and courses (ten weekly 2-hour sessions).

- Posters in local libraries, town halls and other public noticeboards.
- Posters and/or articles in local town, village and parish newsletters.
- Press releases to local newspapers and radio stations.
- Entry in What's On listings on local radio; websites; and local magazines.
- Entry in What's On listings in writing magazines.
- Poster/press release to local writing groups.
- Announcements on social media: Facebook groups and Twitter with appropriate hashtags.

Appendix: Original Questions
What Am I Currently Writing?
- Short stories for magazines (with associated ALCS payment)
- Short stories for competitions

What Else Could I Write?
- Letters and short pieces for magazines
- Short stories for anthologies: (promotion, not earning)
- Non-fiction book relating to library management
- Novel (probably in the steampunk genre)

- Website copy for organisations that use the library (not interested)
- Reports and promotional material for the Town Council (not interested)

Any Other Writerly Activities?
- Talks to WI, U3A and similar groups
- Beginners' Creative Writing courses

Who Will Buy My Writing and My Services?
- Short Stories:
    - Womags in UK: People's Friend; Woman's Weekly; My Weekly; Take A Break
    - Womags in USA: The Sun Magazine; The Threepenny Review
    - Womags in Australia: The Australian Women's Weekly; Quadrant; Woman's Day
    - Womags in Canada: Descant; The Fiddlehead; The Malahat Review; Queen's Quarterly
    - Womags in NZ: Freelance; New Zealand Woman's Day; Takahe
- Competitions launched in UK or internationally
- Letters and short pieces: as per short story markets
- Anthologies where there is a payment or other tangible benefit
- Non-fiction book: specialist publishers

- Novel: speculative at present, no market identified
- Website copy and council reports: will not be pursued, no market identified
- Talks: WI, U3A, Probus, Chambers of Commerce, Business Networks
- Beginners' Creative Writing Course: to members of local writing groups and individuals who are at the start of their writing journey

How Shall I Promote My Writing and Services?
- By building a general platform and raising my profile; establishing myself initially as an expert in short story writing and selling.
- By using a range of specific marketing approaches for the talks, the workshops and the courses.

What Should I Charge?
- For my writing, the fees and prizes are fixed by the client/organiser.
- For the talks, the workshops and the courses, I will carry out market research into the going rate from my competitors and use that as a base.

What Are The Financial Implications?
I will be working three days per week. My salary plus my savings mean I can manage for 3 years without additional income. This gives me a time-frame to establish my business. My aim is

therefore to at least break even in the first year and to be making a positive contribution by the end of year two. By the end of year three, I need to be replacing the salary lost by moving from 5-day to 3-day working.

Figure 2 Business Plan (Business Model Canvas)

Business Plan (Business Model Canvas)

Owner: Anthea Rosewood

Business name: Anthea Rosewood Writes

Business address: Honeysuckle Cottage, Fieldfare Road, Moortown, Devon

Business website: www.anthearosewood.co.uk

Date: 1st January 2018

Customer Segments

1. Readers of Women's magazines in major English-speaking countries (indirectly); editorial staff of said magazines (directly)

2. Organisers of short story competitions

3. Members of WI, U3A, Probus and similar membership groups

4. Local writers, either beginners hoping to become professionals, or amateurs who wish to improve at their hobby

Value Proposition

1. Direct customers need to fill the pages of the magazines each week or month with well-written, appropriate material that will fulfil the expectations of the readers. Indirect customers want to read said material. I have a track record in delivering short stories that tick all the boxes for both direct and indirect customers. I am already offering some of the products; the rest can easily be included in my repertoire.

2. Direct customers need to obtain well-written short stories that comply with all the terms and conditions. I have a track record in delivering short stories that tick all the boxes.

3. Direct customers are the membership secretaries who need to identify suitable speakers for their programmes of (usually) monthly meetings. Speakers should be well-prepared, accomplished speakers, with their own props and equipment, and flexible. Indirect customers are the members who need to be interested in and entertained by the talks. I am used to preparing and giving presentations in the library and have my own laptop and flash drives. I am willing to speak for £50 all in, and do not ask for additional expenses, unless the venue is more than 20 miles from home.

4. I offer one-off 2-hour workshops for customers who are completely new to writing; are not sure if they want to take it further; or cannot commit to more than one session. I also offer a course of ten weekly 2-hour sessions for customers who want to develop their skills in more detail; and want to take on an ongoing activity. In both cases, I am dealing with the writing and submission of short stories, a topic in which I have a track record and an acknowledged level of expertise. The low

numbers of delegates ensures adequate time to devote to each attendee, both during the session and outside of that time frame.

Channels

1. Primarily online, apart from the few UK magazines that still require paper submissions.

2. Online only. Competitions that require hard copy submissions will be ignored.

3. Delivery of the talks will be face-to-face at the venue of the customer's choosing. Generally, this will be within 20 miles of home. Longer journeys will be undertaken with prior agreement.

4. Delivery of the workshops and courses will be face-to-face at venues of my choosing.

Customer Relationships

1. Initial relationship will be formal and professional, using the medium dictated by the publication. Once a track record has been established, I would expect to develop a more informal relationship with specific editors.

2. Initial relationship will be as defined by the organiser of the competition. This will always be electronic and may be automated as well. In the event of a shortlisting or a win, there may be further development of the relationship, if

there are events to attend or promotion to engage in.

3. Where I approach the customer, communication in the first instance will be via email. This may be expanded to include telephone calls once a booking has been made. Where the customer approaches me (as with the WI) communication may be via email or telephone call.

4. Initially, potential customers will contact me via email, telephone, post or website contact form. Booking forms will be available online and to download. Confirmation will be primarily by email or telephone. If booking is made by post, a SAE will be required for confirmation.

Revenue Structure

1. 3 stories per month at an average of £150 per sale; 1 letter or short article per month at an average of £25 per piece; annual ALCS payment of £150. **Total: £5,850**

2. 5 competition wins per year with an average prize of £250. **Total: £1,250**

3. 1 talk to a membership group per month with a fee of £50. **Total: £600**

4. 7 one-off workshops per year with an average of 8 attendees each paying £10; 2 ten-week

courses with an average of 8 attendees each paying £100. **Total: £2,160**

Total income expected in year 1: £9,860

Key Resources

1. No resources required to create value or revenue, apart from my creativity. Resources for distribution are laptop and internet connection for electronic communications; printer/paper/envelopes/stamps for hard copy communications. A system for recording and progressing submissions is required.

2. As for 1. Above.

3. Resources required to create value and revenue include presentation materials and props, plus computer for formal presentations. Resources for distribution are laptop and internet connection for electronic communications plus telephone. A system is required for gathering contact details and keeping them up to date.

4. Resources required to create value and revenue include a suitable venue, training materials and computer. Resources for distribution are laptop and internet connection for electronic communications plus telephone. A system is required for taking bookings and recording customer details.

Key Activities

1. Write short stories, letter and short magazine pieces; submit regularly; monitor responses.

2. Write short stories; submit regularly; monitor responses.

3. Keep presentations updated and bring in new topics when appropriate; get in touch with programme secretaries and other contacts.

4. Write training material and keep it updated; plan workshops and courses; sell places; Deliver sessions

Key Partnerships

1. None

2. None

3. None

4. Venue hirers

Cost Structure

The most expensive resource is the venue for the workshops and courses; the most expensive activity is the hiring of the venues. This aspect of the business is the one presenting the most risk.

1.12 References

Templates and advice from the UK Government can be found here: www.gov.uk/write-business-plan

Small Business Pro is a free UK-based, resource, help and advice site for small business entrepreneurs: www.smallbusinesspro.co.uk/start-business

The US Small Business Administration (SBA) is an independent agency of the federal government established to aid, counsel, assist and protect the interests of small business concerns: www.sba.gov/business-guide/plan/write-your-business-plan-template

Business News Daily has published a list of sources of business plan templates which can be found here: www.businessnewsdaily.com/5067-free-business-templates-word-pdf.html

2. Business Objectives

2.1 Introduction

Recently, a friend asked me how she should deal with multiple projects. How could she sort out what she should be doing first?' My immediate response was she should work on her time management. But my more considered answer was she needed to sort out her objectives first.

Even before attempting to manage our time effectively, we need clear objectives. If we don't have objectives, we don't know what we need to do—and we don't know how we're getting on. Have we exceeded our expectations? Are we just getting along

OK? Or are we getting to the stage where we should think of doing something else?

Incidentally, there is one view of all this planning we're talking about that suggests setting your objectives should come before writing your business plan. That you need an aim, or a Mission Statement, before you start. Or that you should be able to differentiate between your strategy and your tactics. My view is that's the approach taken by large organisations, or consultancies specialising in business terminology. Where the planning becomes an end in itself. My aim, in this series, is to keep it simple and provide you with some basic skills. To identify the questions and suggest some ways of finding the answers. What you call the steps in the process is fairly academic.

For an objective to be helpful, it needs to be written in a certain way. I want to be a successful writer, working away in my cottage in the country with roses around the door. The second part of that objective is clear and measurable—and, as I write this, the roses are just coming into bloom and look spectacular in the early morning sunshine. However, the first part is no help to me at all. What does 'successful' mean? What am I going to write? How will I know when I get there? And please note, I said 'when' rather than 'if'. We'll talk about positivity another time. If your objectives are too vague, too numerous or too unrealistic, they'll get in the way. So, here are my suggestions for setting SMART objectives. It's not an original concept and I don't claim to have invented it. But it's the best system I've found; and it's one I use myself.

2.2 Make it Specific [S]

Work out exactly what you want to achieve. For example: 'to increase the number of magazines buying my articles' or 'to increase the number of ebooks sold' are more specific objectives than 'to increase my level of sales'.

2.3 Make it Measurable [M]

Put a number to it so you will know whether it's achieved or not. For example: 'to sell ten articles to magazines' or 'to deliver six paid workshops' are measurable targets.

2.4 Make it Achievable [A]

You can make your objectives quite tough—it's called having stretch targets and it can push you to achieve more than you expect—but there's no point in setting objectives that you have no hope of meeting. That's just demotivating and a waste of time. For example: 'to increase my output of sold articles from four to twenty in year one' is probably not going to be achievable, whereas 'to increase my output of sold articles from four to eight' may well be.

2.5 Make it Relevant [R]

You're running a business, so your objectives must be relevant to that business. For example: 'to spend ten hours per week posting on the social networks' is specific, measurable and realistic, but unless those postings are aimed at raising your business profile or highlighting your expertise, it's just playing. Now, I'm not saying there's necessarily anything wrong with playing; we all need a bit of fun along the way and some of those kitten pictures are really cute. Just so long as you don't kid yourself you're moving the business forward at the same time.

2.6 Make it Time-related [T]

Have a time-frame for achieving each objective. For example, 'to increase my output of sold articles by 100%' without adding a timescale such as 'in year one' is meaningless. Sure, you can do it at some point, but if you don't have a milestone to work to, it could take ten, fifteen or even thirty years and that's not a particularly stretching objective, is it?

2.7 How Many Objectives Do I Need?

Going back to the question I raised at the start of this chapter, the basis of my friend's query was that she had too much to do and didn't know how to prioritise. And that's something we can probably all recognise; I know I do. We're all trying to fit too much into too short a time.

When I worked in the corporate world, I once had a boss who, when asked which of the twenty items on our To Do list he wanted us to prioritise, insisted on saying 'all of them'! Of course, that wasn't possible, and we continually failed to live up to his expectations. Which was demoralising and bad for our ongoing performance. If he'd understood the need for realistic objectives, life would have been more positive and probably more productive too.

Working for yourself, you often have a stricter boss than if you worked for someone else. I set myself stretch targets every year, and then panic when I realise they aren't all achievable and need to be prioritised. And if you have too many objectives, you're not going to achieve them all. So, it makes sense to sort out the real priorities and concentrate on them. I'm not going to give you a specific number and say: that's the right one. That would be silly. But I would suggest you try to keep it to single figures; maybe even just five or six. Having said that, I've just checked my current objectives list for this year and I have nineteen on there! That could explain why I'm always complaining I'm short of time and have too much to do. So, I'm going to revisit that list and pare it down to a more manageable number.

2.8 Conclusion

If each of your objectives is SMART you'll have a good chance of achieving them and a better way of monitoring progress. Once you've set them, you'll only need to check back every six months or so, just to remind yourself what you're supposed to be doing.

Management by Objectives is a concept that's been around since the 1950s. The acronym SMART has been applied to objectives since the 1980s. There are a few variations in the terms applied to some of the letters, but the ones used above work for me and can be applied to any small business, including writing. Everything you need to apply this concept is given above, but for completeness, references to the original works are given below.

Anthea Rosewood: Objectives

1	To submit 6 short stories per month to a range of women's magazines across the English-speaking world, with a success rate of 50%; selling an average of 3 per month	S √	
		M √	
		A √	
		R √	
		T √	
2	To enter 50 short story competitions during the year, with a success rate of 10%; winning 5 during the year	S √	
		M √	
		A √	
		R √	
		T √	
3	To submit an average of 10 letters or short pieces per month to women's magazines and to achieve a publication success rate of 10%	S √	
		M √	
		A √	
		R √	
		T √	
4	To present an average of 1 talk per month to appropriate membership groups from January 2019 onwards	S √	
		M √	
		A √	
		R √	
		T √	
5	To run a total of seven one-off workshops in Creative Writing during the year, with an average of 8 delegates per workshop	S √	
		M √	
		A √	
		R √	
		T √	
6	To run two short courses in Creative Writing between September 2018 and March 2019, with an average of 8 delegates per course	S √	
		M √	
		A √	
		R √	
		T √	

Figure 3 SMART Objectives

2.9 Worked Examples

On page 42, you can see a set of SMART objectives developed by Anthea Rosewood. For reasons of space, inputs and outputs have been combined in objectives 1-3. An alternative approach would be to split each one into two, since achievement of inputs does not necessarily guarantee achievement of outputs.

2.10 References

The Practice of Management by Peter Drucker; originally published in 1954; latest edition, 2007.

Doran, G. T. (1981). "There's a S.M.A.R.T. way to write management's goals and objectives". Management Review. AMA FORUM. 70 (11): 35–36.

3 Thinking About Finances

3.1 Introduction

In the next section, *Finance Matters,* we will look at finance systems in detail. At this point, we're just going to take a broad-brush approach. One phrase often quoted by experienced business people is: **turnover is vanity; profit is sanity**. The long-term objective of any small business is to be successful; otherwise why do it? And in the context of this chapter, I'm going to define success as profitability. I know that's not by any means the only measure of success for a writer, but today you've got your business owner's hat on, so it needs to be considered.

In all businesses, and writing is a business like any other, there is one important equation:

income minus costs equals profit

The financial advice most appropriate for you as a small business owner will often depend on the stage you've reached in the life-cycle of your business. When you're just starting out your financial priorities and expectations will be different from when you have an established or mature business.

Starting out is an exciting, but also a scary time. You must identify an aspect of your writing that's saleable and which you can deliver; and you may have to experiment or do some development before you get that right. You must identify your potential customers and get the message out to them that you're around. And you need systems in place to make sure you get paid for your writing.

3.2 Interim Funding Options

These activities may take some time to get through and need to be completed before you can expect any income. Therefore, you may need to think about interim funding options.

- Do you need to stay with the day job, which might be completely unrelated to writing, to pay the bills, while establishing yourself as a writer? Can you negotiate reduced hours or days, as a compromise?

- Are there other writerly activities, such as teaching, which you could do to supplement your income?

- Do you have savings or investments you can rely on?

- Are there other members of the family who can help?

- Are there any grants or other types of financial support available? It's always worth investigating the latest government support schemes. And there are all sorts of private funds around that might help with a one-off grant.

- Do you need to take out a bank loan? Personally, I believe the bank loan option should not be one you consider when you are just starting out. It's a mistake to take on an additional financial commitment, such as an interest payment, before you know whether your business will succeed or not.

At this stage, paying yourself a wage is going to be the last thing on the list. If there are staff associated with this business, you have to make sure their wages are paid—even if yours aren't. This would include your support team like child-minders or cleaners you might use to clear your own time for writing.

Despite my opening comments about profitability, at this early stage, just being able to pay the bills and keep the business open can be considered a measure of success. Unless you're very lucky, this is certainly not the time to be thinking about company cars, health insurance or membership of the local golf club.

3.3 Conclusion

Although the long-term aim of a business will normally be to achieve profitability, or at least to break even, this is unlikely to be possible when you are starting out. There is a need to consider interim financial options during the period when you are setting up your writing business and transitioning from being employed to being a business owner. And those interim arrangements need to extend to payment for any support staff you might engage, even if you don't take a salary yourself.

3.4 Worked Example

On page 50, you can see Anthea Rosewood's review of her interim financial options. Having compared proposed income with expected outgoings, she concludes it is possible for her to survive for three years. She plans to review this situation periodically and update here assessment. (We will cover income and outgoings in more detail in the next section, *Finance Matters*.)

Interim Financial Options

Staying in the day job?	Continuing to work in the library but reducing from 5 days to 3 days per week. Salary reduced by 40%, from £35,000 to £21,000.
Other writerly activities?	Expected income from writing activities. £9,860.
Savings or investments?	Savings of £50,000 in ISAs.
Family help?	Not an option.
Grants?	UK government grants and soft loans for business start-up and training purposes
Bank Loan?	Not an option.
Other options?	Downgrade to a smaller car. Take fewer holidays and stay in UK, rather than travelling abroad.

Figure 4 Interim Financial Options

3.5 References

Information about sourcing small business government grants in the UK can be found here: www.startuploans.co.uk/business-advice/get-small-business-government-grant

Information about sourcing small business grants in the US can be found on the Fundera website here: www.fundera.com/blog/small-business-grants

4. Reaching The Customers

4.1 Introduction

Setting up a successful small business is a major step—and is not one you should take lightly. Note my use of the word 'successful'. I'm going to assume your small business will be successful.

For your business to survive, there are ONLY three things that need to happen: you need to get customers; you need to satisfy the demands of those customers; and you need to get paid. Everything else is window-dressing. So, let's start by thinking about those customers and how you're going to find them.

4.2 Types of Customers

If we start by thinking about all the different types of customer a writer might have, we come up with quite a long list, and I'm sure your list would be even longer than mine. For books, whether fiction or non-fiction, the traditional customer is an agent or a publisher. However, with advances in technology and the growth of independent publishing, the reader is much more accessible as a direct customer. Additionally, there are newspapers, journals and magazines, both hard-copy and electronic. Thinking slightly outside the box, every company in the country is publishing something—whether it's the annual report of a major multi-national, or a simple website for the garage down the road—and not all those companies will have the writers they need on the payroll. There are also professional associations, sports organisations; the list goes on and on. Think about your own interests, experiences and expertise: where would you go to find out about any of them? Once you've identified your potential customers, here are some tips for how to reach them.

4.3 Networking Ideas

For people to become your customers, they need to know you exist. Which means, getting your name and contact details out there. Spend as much time networking as you can. Tell everyone you know, and everyone you don't know but just happen to be talking to, that you are a writer. And since these encounters are often quite short—chatting at the bus-stop or waiting for your turn in the supermarket or the pub—make sure you've prepared and practised your elevator speech. That's the two or three sentences telling people who you are, what you have to offer, and how you can be of benefit to them. It should last no more than twenty or thirty seconds, the time it takes for a chance encounter in an elevator; hence the name.

Don't underestimate the size of your indirect network. Each one of your family and friends has their own circle of contacts. Ask them to pass the word around. Next time someone says to them "I wish I could find someone who could..." they might think of you and pass the word on.

Print some simple flyers or business cards and leave them with local shops, restaurants and bars. With today's technology, you can do this yourself, without incurring huge printing costs, and still put over a professional image.

As a writer, you don't have to find customers just around the corner. Having dealt with the local opportunities, it's time to turn to the rest of the big wide world—and that's where the internet comes in. The power of electronic networking was first brought home to me when I joined LinkedIn more than a decade ago; at the time, it was the best option for my professional networking. Initially, I only had 11 contacts of my own. Yet the third-degree network available to me (contacts of my contacts' contacts) was more than 182,000 people. Now, I have more than 1,300 direct contacts and my third-degree network runs into the millions.

Today, the options for electronic networking are much wider—and frankly, can be confusing: blogs, websites, Twitter, Facebook, Google+, Pinterest, Instagram, Snapchat, WhatsApp, Goodreads, YouTube plus others. It's perfectly possible to spend all your time on one or more of these platforms, but that would be counterproductive, as you wouldn't get any writing done. I would suggest you pick two or three and concentrate on those. Currently, most of my effort goes into Facebook and Twitter, but if you are more interested in pictures, then Instagram or Pinterest might be better for you. I do try, however, to have an account on all the social media platforms, as you never know where someone is going to search for you. So, I have lots of passive accounts, with prominent links to my active sites, so I can always be found.

One thing I would say, from experience, is that it's useful to keep a list of all your social media links in one place. Every time you write a guest blog post, a magazine article or a press release, you'll need to give a list of your contact points. Having them all to hand is much simpler than having to go online and copy them all from the live systems each time.

4.4 Making Contact

Make sure you are contactable at all times. The best ways to do this are by email, mobile phone or Direct Messaging via one of the social networking platforms. When you're starting out, you can't afford to be choosy over when you work or when you talk to people. You need to be there when they need you— or you're not there at all.

Establish a presence on the internet. That doesn't mean spending huge amounts of time or money developing an all-singing, all-dancing website. That can come later. For now, all you need is the equivalent of an electronic business card.

Invest a small amount of money in a suitable domain name. It makes the business look bigger than it is and allows you to have a related email address. An address like *mybusiness@gmail.com* is a dead giveaway that you're a small outfit. An address like *myname@mybusiness.com* looks more professional. Use the templates and site-builder software that come with many of the web-hosting services. You can develop a simple, professional-looking site in less than an hour. Several of the blogging platforms can also be used to set up simple websites. See the reference section below for some examples.

4.5 GDPR

The EU General Data Protection Regulation is a wide-reaching law aimed at protecting the personal identifiable information of individuals across the European Union. As of 25th May 2018, there is a legal requirement for compliance with GDPR on all organisations which offer goods or services to, or monitor the behaviour of EU citizens, *wherever those organisations are located.*

In recent years, many people have become concerned about the use and abuse of our personal data and GDPR is a measure to prevent security breaches and loss of data. It puts the individual back in charge of their own data.

As a legal requirement, there are fines associated with non-compliance; and these can be punitive. Some people are predicting the implications for all businesses—micro, small or multi-national—are hugely significant; others believe it's a law aimed either at large companies, or criminals who are abusing or manipulating data; and consequently, the impact on small operations such as your writing business will be minimal.

Frankly, it is too soon to know how GDPR will pan out. At the moment, there's a huge amount of confusion about who needs to do what. And I'm certainly not going to give any legal advice here. That would be inappropriate. However, it is important to note that you need to understand the requirements of GDPR and ensure you are compliant with them, particularly in relation to email distribution lists. This is one area where further professional advice needs to be sought.

4.6 Conclusion

There are only three things you need to do to make a success of your business: find the customers; satisfy their requirements; and get paid. In this chapter, we are looking at the first of those, which involves making the most of your direct and indirect networks, both physical and virtual.

4.7 Worked Example

On page 60, you can see an audit carried out by Anthea Rosewood on her current and potential networks.

4.8 References

Examples of platforms for free websites/blogs can be found here: wordpress.com, www.weebly.com, www.wix.com

Examples of sites offering low cost domain names can be found here: www.1and1.co.uk, www.123-reg.co.uk, www.hostgator.com

Anthea Rosewood: Audit of Networks

My own networks	Friends and family Writing contacts (magazines etc) Library Gym Community choir Local church
Friends and family with networks	Best friend works in local hospital Two friends work in local schools Mother is member of 6 U3A groups Father is member of local golf club
Physical locations for leaflets and business cards	Library Gym Church Local coffee shop Town Hall Information centre Doctor's surgery waiting room Dental surgery waiting room

Figure 5 Audit of Networks

5. Doing The Work

5.1 Introduction

Once you've got your customers, you must satisfy, or preferably exceed their expectations. If you do, they're likely to come back to you next time they need the same service and recommend you to other people. In fact, it's a good idea to ask satisfied customers to pass your name on to their contacts. So here are my tips for getting the work done.

5.2 Where

Any business needs premises from which to work. As writers, we're lucky we can work anywhere, especially in these days of mobile technology. The first consideration should always be to work from home or from the customer's premises. It's the cheapest option and there will be no extra facility costs involved. If you're working from home, you may be able to offset some of your household bills against your income, although this is a tricky area from the point of view of taxation, and it is worth taking professional advice. A good overview of the subject can be found in the *Writers' and Artists' Yearbook*.

If you're unable to work from home, then try to find options other than long-term renting or buying. Maybe there's a local business with spare space they're willing to let you use. They might consider a barter deal, where you provide advertising copy or press releases for them in lieu of rent. Investigate your local libraries or internet cafes. Best-selling author of contemporary romantic fiction, Jenny Kane, who lives here in the Southwest of the UK, spends so long in her local coffee house, they've even put up a plaque to her. And, if you do decide to rent premises, then investigate local schemes which support start-up businesses.

5.3 When

Make sure you have the time to write; and the necessary peace and quiet. This is your job as well as your business and this means it must take priority. You may need back-up systems such as child-care arrangements and may have to consider contracting out housework etc. If you worked for someone else, you wouldn't be able to drop everything each time there was a problem at home; so why should you be expected to do so when you work for yourself?

Especially if you are working from home, make sure people understand you're not available for coffee or chats during your working time. Again, they wouldn't interrupt you if you had a 'proper job', so why should they do it now?

There are all sorts of ways of shutting out potential distractions. I know of some writers who shut themselves away with dire warnings pinned to the door; of others who use ear-plugs to ignore interruptions. Personally, if external noises are disturbing me, I resort to headphones with ear-buds. Even without any music playing, they are sufficient to deaden any sound and ensure I am able to concentrate.

5.4 How

You'll need the right equipment to do the work, or should I say, the appropriate equipment, since not everyone works in the same way. As a writer, your start-up is going to be a lot simpler than if you were setting up, for example, a motor repair shop or even a gardening business. Let's face it, for some of us, the main equipment is a pencil or pen and a shiny notebook!

Even if you do prefer to write long-hand initially, you're going to need a computer at some point, whether it's a desktop, a laptop, a tablet—or whatever device the developers come up with next. A printer of some kind is useful; but whether you choose the slowest, most basic model that only prints in black or the top-of-the-range, colour version, depends on the sort of printing you're likely to be doing. I use a simple black-only one that quickly produces draft quality material when I'm printing out a book manuscript for editing; and a high quality, low speed, full colour model for posters and other promotional material. Of course, not everyone has the space or the finances for more than one printer. Mine are a legacy from a previous business venture. But you can always combine the functions by using your colour printer to produce draft copies in black and white.

The ability to scan documents is useful, for example if you want to convert a hard-copy contract into electronic format for emailing. So, a combined printer/scanner/copier could be a good buy. You probably won't need a fax machine as this technology is almost obsolete; and if you do need to send faxes, there are plenty of low cost electronic options.

Having sorted out your hardware, you will also need to consider software. The basics will include a package for word processing and probably for spreadsheets too. There are reliable options for these, both paid and free. Many writers also use an application like *Scrivener* for organising their projects. We will look at this topic in more detail in the third section of this book, *Improving Effectiveness*. And without a doubt, you will need a reliable, Anti-virus package. There are also free versions of these available, but given the risks to our systems, a paid-for option such as Norton or MacAfee is preferable.

You will certainly need a system for backing up your files. That can be a physical method such as a removable disc drive or data stick; or a virtual method such as Dropbox. In these days of increasing cyber terrorism, it's advisable to have a combination of both. You will need a phone of some kind, so people can get hold of you. And finally, you'll need access to the internet. And that's probably it.

Looking around my office as I type this, I can see filing cabinets, bookshelves, flip-charts, noticeboards and so on; but these are all optional extras I've accumulated over the past twenty-five years. And frankly, some of them are rarely, if ever, used. The basic equipment you need is what I've listed above.

5.5 Just Get On With It

Finally, you need the will to get on and write. So many of us complain of having writer's block; losing the muse; being too busy doing other things; and therefore not getting anything done. At the risk of repeating myself: this is your job, not just your business. Write through the block; use triggers to wake up the muse; stop doing those other things— just get on and write.

5.6 But Don't Forget The Fun

Bearing in mind that writing can be the best job in the world, don't forget to have fun along the way. Otherwise, why be in business for yourself? You might as well go out and get a 'proper job'.

5.7 Conclusion

Once the customers are identified and their requirements understood, it's time to get on with the job. As writers, the choice of venue is diverse, and the start-up equipment requirements are simple. So, there's no excuse. Get on with it; but remember to have fun at the same time.

5.8 Worked Example

On page 69, you can see the review carried out by Anthea Rosewood of her options for a venue in which to work.

Anthea Rosewood: Venue Review

Venue Type	Options
Working from home	Dining Room
	Spare bedroom
Pros	**Cons**
Cheap	Hard to switch off
No travel	Clutters the house
No need for clean desk policy	Restricts use of spare room

Venue Type	Options
Working from client's venue	Not applicable

Venue Type	Options
'Free' space	Own desk in library
	Public desk in library
	Local deli/coffee shop
Pros	**Cons**
Cheap	Unfair on other library staff
No disruption at home	Pulled into library issues
Separates home and work	Coffee shop too noisy

Venue Type	Options
Paid-for space	Serviced office
	Room for rent
Pros	**Cons**
Facilities in serviced office	Rental costs
Peace and quiet	No facilities in room for tent
Separates home and work	6 month minimum contract
No disruption at work	

Figure 6 Venue Review

6. Getting Paid

6.1 Introduction

We've talked about finding the customers; we've looked at getting the work, i.e. the writing, done. Now we're going to focus on the third element: getting paid. Talking about money is something new business owners often find very difficult. However, no-one will think badly of you for charging a fair rate for your work. After all, that's what they're doing, whether they're running businesses themselves or working for someone else. So here are my tips for how to get paid.

6.2 How to get Paid

The first step is back at the beginning before the work is started. The value of a signed contract, preferably to your own format, cannot be stressed too highly. It is important to clarify the obligations both of the supplier, that's you, and your client in advance, thus avoiding problems further down the line. Some clients, such as commissioning editors, will have their own format of contract. Make sure you read it carefully before signing it to ensure you understand all aspects. If in doubt, take professional advice. At the very least, a customer purchase order can be taken as proof of commitment to pay once the work is delivered.

Do make sure you have a system in place to collect money, which means keeping a record of what you've done; invoicing at an appropriate time period: weekly, monthly or at the end of the job; and chasing invoices if they're not paid on time. Otherwise, not everyone will be honest enough to pay up—and that will be very bad for cashflow, not to mention damaging your self-confidence.

Try to negotiate at least some percentage of the money in advance. This is especially important if you must buy materials or incur travel or other expenditure to do the work. However, it's also a way to reduce the risk that you will not get paid. Unfortunately, there are people out there who will take your work and then refuse to pay.

If you suspect there's going to be a problem with payment, then cut your losses and walk away before the job is started. A customer that doesn't pay is not a customer you need, or can afford, to keep. And by the same token, if a customer defaults on a contract, the best course of action may be to learn from the experience and walk away. Litigation can be stressful, very expensive and not necessarily successful.

At the end of the financial year many organizations, particularly public ones, are looking to spend excess budget money, on the 'use it or lose it' basis. So, the last couple of months of the financial year can be a good time to prospect for work. Even if they don't need the work done until the next budget cycle, they may be willing to make an advance payment for services to be supplied later. When we set up our first business, back in 1992, my husband's former employer pre-bought a chunk of his consultancy time. The invoice was raised and paid in March, although the work didn't take place until some months later. Now that's a really good way to 'borrow' money without incurring interest payments.

6.3 Conclusion

Although it may be difficult at first, there is no shame in asking people to pay for the work you do for them, including your writing. And without payment, there is no business. So, it's important to have systems in place for raising invoices and chasing late payments.

6.4 Worked Example

On page 75, you can see the checklist developed by Anthea Rosewood to ensure that she gets paid for each project she completes.

Checklist for Getting Paid

Item	Done	Comments
Requirements, delivery date, fees, payment timing and method agreed with client		
Necessity reviewed for payment in advance		
Option for payment in advance discussed with client		
Pro-forma in place for invoicing		
Methods in place to ensure payment is easy for client: BACS, PayPal, credit card etc?		
Invoice raised at time of delivery		
System in place for chasing outstanding payments immediately after due date is exceeded		

Figure 7 Checklist for Getting Paid

7. Working For Nothing?

7.1 Introduction

If there's one subject that seems to cause more conflict among writers than any other, it's the question of working for nothing. I've seen some quite vicious arguments break out on some of the internet forums each time the question is raised, and writers, we all know how to use our words as weapons.

At the one extreme, there are some people who believe we should never write anything for free; we may be craftspeople, but we still have bills to pay. Publishers and printers all get paid, so why should writers be any different?

At the other extreme, there's a view that we are artists and the words are more important than the money. That we should use any and all opportunities to get our writing published—even if we have to pay for the privilege rather than the other way around.

Personally, I sit somewhere in the middle—and, as always, I'm looking at it from the point of view of a businesswoman as well as a writer. We should never be ashamed to expect payment for our writing. It may take thirty minutes, an hour or a day to write something; but it takes ten, twenty, or maybe more years to learn how to write that something.

However, very few of us only do one type of writing, or writerly work, all the time. We tend to write in different ways for different purposes. For example, here are some of the ways in which you might write.

Most, but not all, further your businesses, although not all of them do so with direct financial returns. The key thing is to understand which is which; and to decide whether each individual piece of work is worth it or not.

7.2 Writing and Financial Returns

Articles for newspapers and journals are generally written on commission. Hence you have a formal or informal contract and an expectation of payment on delivery or on publication. Don't forget to send an invoice with the piece.

Traditionally published non-fiction books and novels by established authors are also generally written on commission. You would expect a formal contract and, if you are lucky, an advance paid at time of contract and/or delivery of the manuscript. Further payment will depend on sales of the book, although you will not be asked to pay back the advance in the unlikely event that the book bombs.

Fiction books by first-timers aiming to follow the traditional publishing route are generally written on spec. We are continually being told this is not the way to a fortune, unless we are very good and very lucky. Hence this would come under the heading of potential financial returns.

Writers following the independent publishing route will generally have to wait until the book is finished and 'out there' before any money arrives. However, on the plus side, the timescales are much shorter than for the traditional route and remain under the writer's control. Payment can be expected on the spot for face-to-face sales of physical books to readers, or within a month to six weeks for sales of ebooks or Print on Demand physical books.

To succeed as a writer these days, we all need to develop our 'platform'. Increasingly this implies engagement with social media plus blogging. Unless you're endorsing a specific product, no-one is going to pay you for writing your own blog, and nor would you expect them to. But if it brings your name to the attention of more potential readers, it is beneficial for your business. Having said that, this book grew out of a series of blog posts, so there's always the option of 'leveraging' further down the line.

Like musicians, writers get better with practice. When I first started writing creatively, I spent some time working on articles for one of the dreaded content mills: those sites which encourage writers to submit pieces with the promise of payment per view, payment that works out at a few pence at most. I never expected to make much money from those articles, and my expectations were not exceeded, but working out how I could improve my writing, and watching my ratings to see what worked and what didn't, was a valuable exercise. It also helped me develop the confidence to put my writing out there.

All businesses need planning and development. We covered planning in an earlier chapter. Development might include writing proposals for articles or books. Not all those proposals will be successful, but the more pitching you do, the 'luckier' you become. You would never expect to get paid for these proposals. I'm always suspicious of anyone who offers me a 'free quotation'; what else should it be but free? But this type of writing is an important part of growing your business.

Writers get all sorts of requests to provide their work for free. And we always have the option of saying no. But sometimes we might want to say yes. I write for and produce *Chudleigh Phoenix*, a small local community magazine. It has no funding, apart from an occasional advertisement, so I don't get paid. But that's my choice. It's my way of giving something back to the community in which I live; and I make sure it doesn't eat into too much of the time I need to devote to my business. I also make sure the readers of the magazine know about my books and short stories as well, so even this 'donated' writing time can benefit the business in some way.

But it's not only our words we're asked to give away for nothing. Our time is also often in demand, as a speaker at a literary festival or a tutor at a workshop. We're told there's no money in the pot to pay writers; we're told there will be a high level of promotion and the resulting exposure will be very valuable for writers, especially if they have a book to promote. Your response to these requests will depend on the circumstances, and the true opportunities you can identify. A new literary festival, especially a local one that accepts independently-published authors, may well have very little funding and will seem deserving of support. In fact, some of you may well be pulled in to organising just such an event, as I am for the annual Chudleigh Literary Festival, now in its eighth year. On the other hand, a larger, more established event, especially one with significant sponsors, should certainly be able to pay expenses, if nothing else.

Another common request is for writers to act as judges of a short story competition. The first time this happened to me, I was flattered and happily accepted. Months later, after reading and commenting on several hundred entries, the free copy of the competition anthology, including my bio and a short article, seemed a poor return for my time and to my knowledge resulted in no additional sales of my books or any benefit to my business. Entrants pay to take part in competitions, and unless it's a charitable exercise, the judges should expect to get a fee, or some kind of compensation for their time and effort.

7.3 ebooks

In the world of independent publishing, it's very common these days to see ebooks offered for free download, either as a short-term promotion, or perma-free. There are lots of reasons you might consider doing this. You might want to revitalise the promotion of a book when sales have slowed down post-launch. You might want to use the first book in a series to introduce readers to your work and hopefully encourage them to buy the rest of the series. Or you might want to provide a give-away in exchange for email addresses to add to your list, although to do so post-GDPR is fraught with pitfalls.

For now, suffice it to say, the success or otherwise of these approaches varies, depending on whom you talk to, the type of book, and the level of promotion applied. And it's worth bearing in mind that the market is continually changing and what worked for one person twelve months or two years ago might be totally ineffective today. There is also a growing feeling that many free ebooks sit, unread, on Kindles and other ereaders all over the world. And if they aren't read, they have no chance of affecting your business in any way at all.

7.4 Conclusion

Not all writing will result in immediate, or even any, financial reward. Sometimes, our work will take the form of unpaid business development or promotional writing. This is an inevitable cost of doing business. However, there are continual requests, or even demands, for writers to provide their work or their time for nothing, with only a promise of 'visibility' as reward. There is no compunction for a writer to agree to these requests and each one should be considered on its merits and assessed for the benefits to your business. An audit of the time spent on paid versus unpaid activities might be useful for that assessment process. As would be a discussion with other writers who have gone down the same road previously.

The use of free ebooks as a marketing and promotional tool is a valid approach, although there are a variety of views as to its success.

7.5 Worked Example

On page 86, you can see a template developed by Anthea Rosewood to monitor the proportion of her time spent on different types of activity, including unpaid work. The definitions are as follows:

1. Unpaid but with expectation of benefit within a year of less;

2. Unpaid but with expectation of benefit in more than a year's time;

3. Unpaid and with no expectation of benefit at any time;

4. Necessary admin work related to the business.

Time Start	Time Stop	Activity	Paid	Unpaid S/T (1)	Unpaid L/T (2)	Unpaid (3)	Admin (4)	Total

Figure 8 Activity Audit Timesheet

8. Business Structures

8.1 Introduction

One of the questions to be resolved when setting up any small business is which structure is the most appropriate? There are several options including: self-employment, also called sole trading or sole proprietorship; partnerships; limited liability partnerships or limited liability corporations; and limited companies, also called corporations. The terminology is based on the UK and US systems; there will be similar options in other countries, although the names may vary. In this chapter, I'm going to look at the first and the last of these, as the two options most independent writers would consider when putting their writing on a business footing. And I'm going to discuss the UK first, then move on to talk about the US. The latter is more complex than the former due to the need to consider both federal and individual state requirements.

8.2 Business Structures in the UK

Key points of self-employment, also called sole trading, in the UK are as follows:

- There is no financial separation between the individual and business; the legal entity is the writer/sole trader;

- There are no formal positions in the company;

- There is a need for registration with the tax authorities within 3 months of starting trading;

- Tax on earnings is paid through Self-Assessment and National Insurance;

- Personal drawings, also called salary, are taken after tax has been deducted.

Key points for a limited company in the UK are as follows:

- The company is a stand-alone business entity with finances separated from the individual; the legal entity is the company, not the writer;

- The company needs at least one shareholder and one director, although these can be the same person; a company secretary is no longer mandatory;

- The company must be registered at Companies House, to whom Annual Returns must be made, plus with the tax authorities;

- Individuals, including directors, are employees and are paid salaries from pre-tax profits;

- Individuals' income tax is paid through the PAYE system;

- Dividends are paid after corporation tax is deducted.

8.3 Business Structures in the US

Key points of sole proprietorship, in the US are as follows:

- There is no financial separation between the individual and business; the legal entity is the writer/sole proprietor;

- There are no formal positions in the company;

- If trading under anything other than the proprietor's real name, there is a need for registration of the Doing Business As (DBA) name via the county clerk or state government, depending on location;

- Tax on earnings is paid through normal Internal Revenue Services (IRS) individual taxation;

- An Employer Identification Number (EIN) is not required for a sole proprietor but is required if there are any employees in the business;

- Personal drawings, also known as salary, are taken after tax has been deducted;

- There may be a need for business licences and permits, but this will vary with activities and location.

Key points for a corporation in the US are as follows:

- The corporation is a stand-alone business entity, sometimes referred to as a legal person, with finances separated from the individual; the legal entity is the corporation, not the writer;

- The DBA name must be registered with the state government;

- The corporation is set up using a document referred to as the Articles of Association. Since these describe the activities of the corporation, it is common practice to keep them brief and general. Making them too specific can restrict the ability to amend activities going forward. Specifics can be covered in the by-laws which can be amended internally by the directors;

- The corporation needs at least one shareholder, one director and officers who would typically be President, Secretary and Treasurer or Chief Financial Officer, although these can usually be the same person;

- The company must be registered with the relevant state, to whom Annual Statements/Reports must be made, plus with the IRS;

- The handling of taxation depends on the type of corporation established. The standard C corporation pays tax at corporate rates on net earnings. Salaries of directors, officers and employees are deductible for the corporation, then taxed via the individuals. However, dividends are taxed both within the corporation and via the individual, double taxation in effect. Therefore, small corporations (such as your writing business) have the option of taking up S corporation status, whereby no taxation is paid within the business, but is all done via the individual. Hence from a taxation point of view, it is like sole proprietorship.

8.4 Pros and Cons of Each Option

The advantages of self-employment or sole proprietorship include it being a cheaper option with less administration and possible benefits such as the availability of free banking in the UK. The disadvantages include the fact that all the assets, both personal and business, are at risk and it may be more difficult to raise finances if required. Additionally, since it is based on one individual, there is no residual value and the business ceases on death.

The advantages of a limited company or corporation include separation, and therefore some protection, of personal assets. This is particularly beneficial in a litigious environment, such as that existing in the US, and increasingly also in the UK. It also presents the possibility of an enhanced image with potential clients. The disadvantages include increased levels of administration and higher costs.

8.5 Conclusion

The choice that any writer makes on business structure will depend on their individual circumstances. By the time I became a full-time writer in 2012, I had run a limited company for twenty years, associated with our technical consultancy work, and simply added my writing to the mix. My systems were established and simple to operate. For me, it was the natural choice. That would not necessarily be the obvious route for a new business. And in fact, when we closed the consultancy in 2016, I transferred to self-employed status for my writing and simplified my systems in the process.

As sorting out the business structure is such a critical aspect of setting up a business, I'm going to repeat the health warning once more: seeking professional advice should be a prerequisite to taking any steps, whether you consult the relevant government or state authorities, a business support organisation or a commercial operation such as an accountant or a lawyer.

8.6 Worked Example

On page 96, you can see a cost-benefit analysis carried out by Anthea Rosewood to determine the most appropriate business structure for her.

8.7 References

Templates and advice from the UK Government can be found here: www.gov.uk/browse/business

Small Business Pro is a free UK-based, resource, help and advice site for small business entrepreneurs: www.smallbusinesspro.co.uk/start-business

The US Small Business Administration (SBA) is an independent agency of the federal government established to aid, counsel, assist and protect the interests of small business concerns: www.sba.gov/business-guide

Anthea R: CBA Self-employment/sole proprietorship

Cost	Score	Benefit	Score
No separation of business and personal assets and finances	-1	Less administration and bureaucracy	2
Possible difficulty of raising finance	-1	Lower costs for administration	2
No residual value; business dies with individual	0	Free banking and other support systems	1
Other costs (list)		Other benefits (list)	
Total costs	**-2**	**Total benefits**	**5**

Anthea R: CBA Limited company/corporation

Cost	Score	Benefit	Score
Higher level of administration and bureaucracy	-3	Separation of business and personal assets	1
Higher costs to operate the business	-2	Enhanced image with clients	1
Other costs (list)	0	Residual value; business can be inherited	1
		Other benefits (list)	
Total costs	**-5**	**Total benefits**	**3**

Scoring System

Assessment	Cost	Benefit
Not applicable	0	0
Of minor importance	-1	1
Of medium importance	-2	2
Of high importance	-3	3

Figure 9 Business Structure Cost-Benefit Analysis

9. Tax Matters

9.1 Introduction

In my experience, no-one likes paying taxes. If there's anyone out there who disagrees with this, get in touch and we'll debate the question. However, it's the law of any land that if you earn money, you have to pay tax on it. I was once berated by an angry writer who said: 'but it's only a hobby'. I'm afraid the tax authorities don't generally recognise the distinction. But in your case, your writing is a business, not a hobby, so there's no question about it: you need to understand your country's tax systems as they apply to you.

This is just an overview of the topic. For detailed information, consult an accountant or go direct to the relevant authority. A list of links is given in the reference section at the end of this chapter. Here in the UK, I find the HMRC website very useful; better still, ring one of the specific helplines. Similarly, for US businesses, the IRS website contains a wealth of information.

9.2 Taxation in the UK

There are four main types of tax to think about: Income Tax, Corporation Tax, Value Added Tax (VAT) and National Insurance.

Income Tax

- This tax is paid on our income, after deduction of expenses and tax-free allowances;

- It applies to everyone. Employees (including directors) of limited companies pay via the PAYE system, in monthly amounts. Self-employed people pay via the self-assessment system and usually make two payments per year;

- There are different rates of tax, depending on income.

Corporation Tax

- This is the tax on company profit after all expenses, including salaries, pension contributions etc have been made;

- This tax only applies to limited companies; it's paid annually in retrospect following completion of the annual tax return;

- There are different rates of tax, depending on the level of profit, but no tax-free allowance.

Value Added Tax (VAT)

- If a company or a self-employed individual is registered for VAT, they must charge it on all applicable sales made;

- VAT registration is mandatory above a certain income level (currently £85,000 in the UK); and while that is not likely to worry many of you

99

during the start-up phase of your business, it is important to know that VAT registration is optional at any level of income;

- VAT is charged at different rates for different goods and services (20%, 5%, and 0%). Physical books are zero-rated, although ebooks are not; see below for a discussion of VAT on digital services. Other writerly activities such as giving talks or leading workshops are charged at 20%.

- If a company or an individual is registered, VAT must be charged on invoices;

- But (and this is probably the most important point in this whole section) if a company or an individual is registered, VAT paid out on business expenses can be claimed back from HMRC;

- This means if you are registered for VAT and only selling physical books, your sales incur a zero rate—so no downside for your customers—but all VAT you pay on stationery, printer cartridges, office furniture etc. can be claimed back;

- There are special schemes to make administration of VAT simpler, depending on the size of the business (measured by gross income level).

National Insurance

- This is the tax that builds your entitlement to certain benefits including state pension;

- Class 1 contributions are paid by both employed earners and their employers within the PAYE system; this is a big expense and is possibly the biggest disadvantage of setting up as a limited company;

- Class 2 (an initial flat-rate) and Class 4 (additional rate, based on level of profit) contributions are paid by the self-employed;

- Class 3 contributions are voluntary payments made to plug gaps in your NI record;

- There are exemptions available for anyone on low earnings, but these need to be applied for, not assumed;

- Payment of NI contributions ceases at state retirement age, even if you continue working.

9.3 Taxation in the US

There are five general types of business taxes to think about: income tax, estimated taxes, self-employment tax, employment taxes and excise tax.

Income tax

- Businesses must file an annual income tax return;

- Federal taxes are based on Pay-As-You-Go;

- Employees, including directors, will usually have income tax withheld from their pay;

- An alternative method is via estimated taxes (see below);

- Rates will vary with level of taxable income;

- Any outstanding tax is paid at the time of filing the return.

Estimated Taxes

- Sole proprietors, shareholders and corporations will generally make regular payments of estimated taxes during the year.

Self-employment tax (SE tax)

- SE tax is a social security tax paid by sole proprietors;

- Social security coverage provides retirement benefits, disability benefits, survivor benefits, and hospital insurance (Medicare) benefits.

Employment taxes

- Employers, whether sole proprietors or corporations, have responsibility to pay and file returns for certain taxes relating to their employees;

- Employment taxes include: social security and Medicare taxes; federal income tax withholding; federal unemployment tax.

Excise taxes

- These relate to specific types of industries and activities, such as transport and betting;

- They are unlikely to apply to a writing business, but if in doubt, expert advice should be sought.

State and Local Taxes

- Most states and some local governments also raise taxation on net income;

- The requirements will vary with jurisdiction and specific advice should be sought.

9.4 EU Sales of Digital Services

Earlier in this chapter, we looked at VAT as one of the elements of taxation in the UK, primarily from the point of view of a UK business selling into the UK market. Sales outside of the UK complicate matters, and different rules apply depending on whether the customer is located in an EU member state or a non-EU country. But generally, the point of taxation is the location of the seller, i.e. in the UK, and there is only one set of rules to apply in each circumstance.

However, since January 2015, the situation for sales of digital services to consumers has been greatly complicated by an EU ruling that the point of taxation is the location of the consumer. Which means charging differential rates of VAT and reporting of sales and related taxation to up to 27 separate tax authorities, depending where you make your sales. Ebooks are defined as being digital services and are therefore subject to this ruling, although some training delivered electronically, such as webinars, is excluded.

An additional complication is that there is no registration threshold for digital services. All ebooks sold directly to consumers (i.e. non-businesses) must include VAT at the rate of the state in which the consumer is located.

Following huge levels of disquiet within the UK writerly world, HMRC established VAT Mini One

Stop Shop (VAT MOSS), a system which simplifies the reporting requirements to a single quarterly filing to HMRC who will then handle onward communication with the other Member States.

At the time of writing, the UK is in the middle of Brexit negotiations, so it's not known what the eventual situation will be. However, it's probably safe to assume that leaving the EU is unlikely to totally eliminate the complications.

Due to this situation, the selling of ebooks directly from your website to consumers across the EU has become a highly complex and time-consuming activity for UK writers. However, if you are selling ebooks via Amazon or one of the other distribution platforms, they charge VAT and handle the administration for you. This brings you into the realm of the US IRS and it is necessary to make sure you are correctly registered with them, in order to avoid paying double taxation on your sales. But this is the lesser of two evils and consequently, has pretty much become the default method for UK authors.

9.5 Conclusion

All businesses, whatever their structure, are subject to taxation. The type and level of taxation will depend on several variables including geographic location of the business (and sometimes of the customer as well); business structure in operation; and level of income.

Failure to pay taxes will have consequences for your business, which may be very severe. It is critical to understand the rules and requirements related to your own situation and to have systems in place to comply with those requirements. This is an area where professional advice is recommended.

9.6 References

Guidance from the UK Government on money and taxation can be found here: www.gov.uk/browse/tax

Guidance from the US Government on money and taxation can be found here:
www.irs.gov/businesses/small-businesses-self-employed/business-taxes

10. Who You Gonna Call?

10.1 Introduction

You've identified your business objectives and made your plans; you've decided on your business structures; you've set up your financial systems (and if you need more help with this, see the next section, *Finance Matters*). Now is the time to start thinking about your support network—and we all need one of those.

Writing is a lonely business! You spend hours hunched over a notepad or a keyboard, often staring at acres of white space; and when the page or the screen is full of words, you look at them and wonder if they're any good or whether you're wasting your time. At other times, with your business hat on, you stare at the spreadsheet, the cashbook, or the carrier bag full of receipts, and try to work out what it all means, and why you're doing it.

In most businesses, there would be other people you could talk to; performance standards to measure yourself against; even rules and regulations you could follow. But your business isn't like that. And there will be times when it will all seem too difficult to carry on. But it's your business! You can't just stop doing it—or at least, you shouldn't need to!

10.2 Online Networks

So, you need a support network, and the best place to start looking for this is online. There are many established writing communities on Facebook, Twitter, LinkedIn, Google+ and any other network you might be using. And the beauty of social media is that if you can't find what you want, you can set it up for yourself. Whether you think you will get support from old college friends, from business people in your own town, or from someone across the world, it's all possible via the internet. In fact, I've been chatting, I mean talking business, with a colleague who has become a friend, in Australia just this morning.

10.3 Face-to-Face Networks (General)

When I started my small business more than twenty years ago, the internet wasn't available—at least not for ordinary people—so all our networking was done face-to-face. Even today, when we are all connected and online, some of us far more than we should be, it's still good to get out there and talk to people. A smiley face emoji is no substitute for the real thing.

But remember you're a business owner now and, as such, some of your problems will be shared by people in totally different fields of work. Most towns have general business networks, whether they're called business guilds, chambers of commerce or something more fanciful. For example, here in the Southwest of England, we used to have the wonderfully named Ladies Do Latte, a group of 400+ businesswomen.

Networking groups provide the opportunity to pick the brains of people who will have the same business issues as you, even if their product or service is totally different. And of course, there is always the chance of picking up new projects while chatting to someone over breakfast or lunch.

10.4 Writers' Groups

Local writers' groups are great for helping to improve your writing craft; for critiquing; and for finding like-minded people to share a stall at a book fair, collaborate on a writing project, or act as beta readers. I'm a long-time member of two such groups and they're an important part of my own support network.

But there are many other opportunities for writers to get together, whether that's via national organisations such as the Society of Women Writers and Journalists (SWWJ) and the Romantic Novelists Association (RNA) or more regionally-based ones. All these groups have meetings, which range from annually to monthly. The London Book Fair has traditionally been an industry event, focused on the agents and publishers more than the authors. However, with the growth in indie publishing, this is becoming another useful place to meet people. Six years ago, it was the location for the launch of the Alliance of Independent Authors. ALLi is a thriving community, both online and face-to-face, with a strong belief that we are all business people and providing the support that we need, either as beginners or further on down the line.

10.5 Conferences

Each year I attend one or two writers' conferences and if there is one memory that's stronger than any other, it's the sight and sound of hundreds of writers talking, swapping notes, and learning from each other.

I'm going to give a plug for my favourite, the Swanwick Writers' Summer School. This runs for a week during August, has been doing so for the past 70 years and has a dedicated 'family' of writers who return each year. They're very welcoming to any newcomers or 'white badgers' as they're known and are always willing to help with problems anyone has, either with the craft of writing or with the business side. Of course, I might be biased, as I teach *The Business of Writing* at Swanwick most years, but if you're looking to spread or set up your informal face-to-face network, then a conference is a great way of doing it.

10.6 Professional Support

Having talked about informal networks and especially the support we can get not just from the writing community but also from other small businesses, we're now going to think about the support you might need from the professionals.

When I talk to writers about the financial aspects of their business, I always place emphasis on simple, appropriate systems and preferably low-cost options. However, it's very likely you will need to use an accountant at some point, especially if you have a limited company or corporation. Accountants, or should I say accountancy firms, come in all shapes and sizes, from the local one-man/woman bands to the larger practices with many partners. In general terms, the smaller the practice, the lower the cost, but also the narrower the expertise and experience available. When we started our company more than twenty years ago, we used a small local accountancy firm. It was simple, like our affairs. However, as the business grew and moved into more complex areas of finance—just how *do* you deal with a tax demand from Kazakhstan?—we moved to another practice with more partners and the right experts for our business. It's most important that your accountant, or indeed anyone else you turn to for advice, understands your business.

As well as financial support, you may well need legal advice on occasion, for example when you are setting up your business, signing contracts or drafting your will. The obvious option, and one that many businesses will use, is to engage a lawyer. However, that is not a low-cost solution and there are alternatives that can be explored. In the UK, there is the Business Support Helpline which provides a quick response service for simple questions about starting or running a business or a more in-depth service for complex enquiries. Some of the available portals and services in the UK and the US have been referenced in earlier chapters and are listed once more at the end of this chapter. I've often found the answer to a specific tax query on the HMRC website.

In the UK, there is the Citizens' Advice Bureau which would be able to provide support to individuals, but probably not to limited companies. Or there are business support organisations like the Federation of Small Businesses in the UK and the NFIB in the US which provide members with legal and financial advice. As writers, we have our own support via the Authors Guild in the US, the Society of Authors in the UK, the Alliance of Independent Authors or the National Union of Journalists which can help members with queries relating to the business of writing. Services include the confidential, individual vetting of contracts, and help with professional disputes.

10.7 Conclusion

No matter how well organised you are, or how successful your business, there will be times when you need to talk to someone else, either for informal networking or professional support and advice.

Whatever your query or problem, there will be someone who can help you, either free of charge or as a paid service, depending on the circumstances. It's worth being aware of all these services, so you can call on them rapidly if you need to.

10.8 References

Alliance of Independent Authors:
allianceindependentauthors.org/?affid=366

Authors Guild: www.authorsguild.org/

Citizens' Advice Bureau: www.citizensadvice.org.uk

Federation of Small Businesses: www.fsb.org.uk

HMRC website: www.hmrc.gov.uk

London Book Fair: www.londonbookfair.co.uk

National Federation of Independent Business (NFIB): www.nfib.com/

National Union of Journalists: www.nuj.org.uk/home

Romantic Novelists Association: www.rna-uk.org

Society of Authors: www.societyofauthors.net

Society of Women Writers and Journalists: www.swwj.co.uk

Swanwick Writers' Summer School: www.swanwickwritersschool.org.uk

UK Government: www.gov.uk

US Government: www.usa.gov

Section 2: Finance Matters

11. Keeping It Appropriate

11.1 Introduction

Every business needs to keep records and your writing business is no different from any other in that respect. It's not very creative and, for most people, it's not much fun—although there are some people, like me, who find numbers fascinating and enjoy playing with columns of figures—but it must be done. So, the trick is to have a good system and keep it up to date. That way it takes minimal time and leaves you free to get on with what you really want to be doing—writing.

For a system to be good, it needs to be appropriate. In other words, it needs to have the right level of complexity and no more. There are several options for how you keep your records: a paper system based on handwritten ledgers; a simple electronic system based on a spreadsheet; and a purpose-built system based on commercial software. The choice will often be linked to your type of accounting method; accrual versus cash accounting: and your approach to bookkeeping; single entry versus double entry. And these decisions in turn will be connected to your choice of business structure. Let's start with a few definitions and rules, before looking at the pros and cons of each record keeping system.

11.2 Accounting Methods

The default method used for accounting of transactions is called accrual accounting. Under this system, income and expenditure are recorded at the point they are incurred, rather than when the money is transferred. Sales are recorded at the date of invoice, even if payment is not expected for thirty days or more. Similarly, expenditure is recorded when an invoice is received from your supplier, even if you're not going to pay it straight away. The benefits of this method include a better picture of your overall financial position. But the disadvantages are that it's complicated and can be confusing; it is also harder to determine an accurate picture of cashflow.

An alternative, simpler method is called cash accounting. Under this system, all transactions are recorded at the time money changes hands. Invoices may be raised at the time work is delivered, but no income can be recorded until the bill has been settled. Similarly, expenditure is only recorded once a bill has been paid, no matter how old the invoice is. The advantage of this method, in addition to its simplicity, is the clearer picture you have of your cashflow; and this can be critical to your survival. After all, you can't feed yourself with an unpaid invoice. However, it's much harder with cash accounting to get the full picture of how your business is doing.

In the UK, cash accounting is available to the self-employed and to partnerships, providing their annual income is below £150,000. It is not an option for limited companies.

In the US, cash accounting is available to sole proprietors, to partnerships and to S corporations; but also, to C corporations with an annual turnover of below $5million.

11.3 Bookkeeping Systems

The default method used for bookkeeping is double entry, which is based on the equation:

$$\textbf{Assets = Liabilities + Equity}$$

Some students of bookkeeping have gone cross-eyed trying to understand this system, and I'm not going to spend very long on this, partly because this isn't an accountancy text-book and partly because any business using this system will be doing so with a piece of commercial software. In which case, you need to know how to use it, rather than how it works.

Briefly, the system is set up as a series of accounts relating either to assets or liabilities. Every entry in an account will be balanced by an equal and opposite entry in another account. For example: if you buy some office equipment and you pay the supplier's invoice from your bank account, a debit is made against the asset account (which has gone up), while a credit is made against the bank account (which has gone down). The advantage of this system is that it provides a high level of information about your accounts and therefore allows management of finances at a more detailed level. However, it is complex, time-consuming and, as stated above, will generally involve the use of commercial software.

A simpler method available under some circumstances is single entry bookkeeping, which is based purely on payments into and out of the bank account. It's closely linked to cash accounting. There's no need to track fixed assets or inventories. In this case, each transaction is recorded as a single line entry. This can be done within a single record, but I have always found it easier to keep individual accounts of income and expenditure; compiling them at the year end in the profit and loss account. The advantages lie in its simplicity and low technological requirements. However, the level of detail available is much reduced.

In the UK and the US, there is no legislation regarding which system is used. However, single entry bookkeeping is more suited to the self-employed, partnerships and small businesses. Once the business grows, or if it deals with manufacturing and thus has inventory to account for, double entry becomes the better option.

Regulations vary on a national basis and even within the European Union, different member states have different requirements. This is one of those areas where professional advice needs to be taken before making decisions.

11.4 Paper-Based Systems

This type of system is only really suitable for cash accounting. When we started our own company, back in the 1990s, we set up a paper-based system. It had been in use for several centuries by that point, and we hadn't quite reached the stage where computerisation was the first choice for everything. It was simple to keep but became laborious when the number of transactions increased. The books needed to be completed in ink, as they were legal documents, and hence it was impossible to correct mistakes neatly. I recognise this would not be a problem for everyone, but the sight of crossings-out on an otherwise neat page of figures offended the Virgo in me. For anyone with just a small number of transactions and a dislike of computers, a paper system is a perfectly acceptable option. But the chief disadvantage is the necessity to do all the sums manually. Even those clever folks at Apple have yet to invent a physical book that can add and subtract on its own.

11.5 Commercial Software

At the other end of the scale, there is the system based on commercial software. Once a business reaches any level of complexity, I believe this is a necessity. By complexity I mean, for example, any of the following:

- VAT registration (and in the earlier section, *Business Start-Up*, I talk about why this might be an advantage, even for someone with low levels of income); and from 2019, all VAT returns must be submitted digitally.

- PAYE, either for yourself or an employee (again in *Business Start-Up*, I discuss the different business structures on offer and the pros and cons of each one);

- Stock-holding including copies of your books (since under the accrual system, the costs of printing cannot be claimed against tax until a book is sold);

- Using double-entry bookkeeping and/or accrual accounting.

In my company, we moved to a computerised commercial package towards the end of the 1990s, going with Sage, the best-known company at the time, and still one of the major players. They upgraded their software most years; but we only upgraded ours every few years. As you would expect from a product used across many industries by organisations of all different sizes, there is a huge level of functionality, much of which was not relevant to our business, so I just ignored that and used the bits I needed.

These days, there are a number of options for simplified online accounting packages, including Intuit's QuickBooks which is a paid-for product with a regular monthly fee. There is also an open source product, GnuCash, which can be downloaded and used for free.

11.6 Spreadsheets

I've left the mid-range option until last, as this is probably the one most start-up businesses would go with, and it's the method our guide, Anthea Rosewood is going to use as she continues along her journey towards a full-time writing business. Anyone with a reasonable knowledge of spreadsheets (whether Excel, Works Spreadsheet, or Open Office) can set up simple records. They're really an extension of the paper system with the advantage that the sums are done for you.

In 2016, we closed our limited company as all our technical consultancy activities had ceased. I moved over to self-employment/sole proprietorship for my writing and publishing activities. At the same time, I shut down the commercial software package as its benefits no longer outweighed its complexity for me. I set up a system of simple spreadsheets, recording income and expenses, invoices and stock control. At the end of the year, I'm able to develop a profit and loss statement in preparation for my tax return. It's a perfectly adequate system for my much-simplified business.

Whichever system is most appropriate, it helps no end to keep it up to date, and I would suggest at least a monthly session, or maybe even weekly. Memory is a tricky thing, whatever your age, and trying to remember why you took a taxi on a particular day nine or ten months ago, or whether someone paid cash for a copy of your book sold last year, is time-consuming and not always successful. If you fill in the records at the time, it's quicker and easier—and you're then free to forget the details. I keep a small notebook with me at all times, in which I record all business-related transactions on a daily basis. I then use this 'raw data' to update my spreadsheets periodically.

11.7 Alternative Approach

Of course, there is a fourth option used by some people: throw everything into a carrier bag or shoe-box and then hand it to the accountant at the end of the year with a winsome smile. But that's an expensive option (the clue is in the word 'accountant') and will still involve time spent trying to answer questions and dredge your memory for missing information. It's not an option I would recommend.

11.8 Purpose of These Systems

Having looked at the common types of financial system used by small businesses, whether paper-based, a simple spreadsheet, or commercial software, we're now going to think about the data you'll keep within those systems and start by asking the question: what records do you need to keep?

Well, at its simplest, you need to know what money came in (your income) and what money went out (your expenditure). The difference between the two is your profit or loss. If your income is greater than your expenditure, you've made a profit. However, if your expenditure is greater than your income, you've made a loss.

11.9 Conclusion

Every small business needs finance systems. These systems should be appropriate to the type and size of business. There are several options for record keeping, each of which has pros and cons. Similarly, there are different options for accounting and bookkeeping methods chosen. Reviewing the pros and cons, based on your own circumstances, will help ensure you choose the system most appropriate for your business. Seeking professional advice may also be necessary at this point.

11.10 Worked Example

On page 134, you can see a cost-benefit analysis carried out by Anthea Rosewood to determine the most appropriate systems for her business. The scoring system used is the same as that on page 96.

11.11 References

Templates and advice from the UK Government can be found here: www.gov.uk/browse/business

Small Business Pro is a free UK-based resource, help and advice site for small business entrepreneurs: www.smallbusinesspro.co.uk/start-business

The US Small Business Administration (SBA) is an independent agency of the federal government established to aid, counsel, assist and protect the interests of small business concerns: www.sba.gov/business-guide

Anthea R: CBA Cash versus Accrual Accounting (1)

Cost	Score	Benefit	Score
Turnover must be below a specified level	0	Simpler to understand	2
Full picture of business success harder to determine	-1	Lower costs for administration	2
Only available to sole proprietors (in UK; not in US)	0	Good for monitoring cashflow	2
Not available if you maintain inventory (in US; not in UK)	0	Allows for single entry bookkeeping	2
Total costs	**-1**	**Total benefits**	**8**

Note 1: Since the only alternative to cash accounting is accrual accounting, the analysis can be done just once. If the score for cash accounting is negative, the only option is to use accrual accounting.

Anthea R: CBA Method of Recording

Paper		Spreadsheet		Software	
No tech	0	Low level tech	2	Med level tech	-1
No tech skills	0	Med tech skills	2	Med tech skills	2
Cheap	2	Cheap	2	More costs	-2
Manual set-up	-2	Easy set-up	2	Accrual set-up	-2
Manual calc	-3	Auto calc	3	Auto calc	3
Medium time requirement	1	Low time requirement	2	Medium time requirement	1
Simple business	0	Simple business	0	Any business	1
Total score	**-2**		**13**		**2**

Figure 10 Accounting Methods Analysis

12. Recording Income

12.1 Introduction

In this chapter, we're going to look at the first of the two major transactions within a business. Income is the money that's paid to you as a result of the work you deliver to a customer. And we'll start by considering where that income might come from.

But before we do, I'd like to mention tax; or rather, not mention it. This chapter deals with income and some of that income will be taxable, some may not be. But no distinction is made here between the two and the tax implications are not addressed. That's another of those areas where professional advice needs to be sought.

12.2 Income Streams

As a writer, your income can come from lots of different sources. Here are a few I thought of and there will be others you can list too:

- Sales of your books, either to bookshops or direct to readers;

- Sales of articles or short stories to magazines, journals or websites;

- Prizes from writing competitions;

- Fees for running workshops or courses on writing;

- Advance payments and royalties from publishers;

- Payments through PLR (Public Lending Rights), relating to books borrowed from libraries;

- Payments through ALCS (Authors' Licensing and Collecting Society), relating to photocopying.

Most of these payments will come in as cheques or directly into the bank, so there's an immediate paper trail. Others will tend to come as cash, especially the direct sales of books. Some, particularly the bottom three on the list, will come with full statements.

The two classic ways to document income are by issuing an invoice, which is a demand for payment; or by issuing a receipt, which is a record of payment received, and also the buyer's proof of payment. Some companies issue both for the same transaction, although this is not necessary.

12.3 Invoices

There is no standard format for an invoice, but some pieces of information must be present:

- Date of the transaction;

- Invoice number;

- The seller's name, contact details and VAT number (if applicable);

- The customer's name and contact details;

- Description of the goods or services being sold;

- The net price, any discounts applied, rate of VAT and amount of VAT (if applicable), and the final gross amount to be paid.

And talking about VAT, there's one important point which should be obvious; but which I'll make anyway: if you are NOT registered for VAT, then you must not charge VAT on your invoices.

If the customer has provided you with an order number, then it's a good idea to include that on the invoice, especially when dealing with larger organisations, where the person commissioning the work is not the person paying the bill.

Some invoices also carry details of: customer account numbers; order number; payment terms and instructions on how to pay (who to make the cheque out to; or bank details for direct transfers). The back of the invoice can be a useful space for advertising or getting other messages directly to your customers; for example, these days our utility bills and credit card statements come stuffed with additional information.

There's no standard system for numbering invoices. Some people incorporate the date into their numbering and start again at the beginning of each financial year: 2018/001, 2018/002 and so on. I use a single sequential set of numbers, prefixed with I for invoice: I001, I002 and so on. The invoice number is recorded on my spreadsheet and I file the paperwork in number order, rather than date order. That way, it's easier to tie account entries with the supporting paperwork in case of a query.

If you have a system for issuing invoices, you also need a way of recording when those invoices are paid; and even more critically, of maintaining visibility of unpaid invoices. However, from the point of view of the buyer, the invoice is sufficient record, so there is no need to issue a receipt against payment of an invoice unless you want to.

12.4 Receipts

Receipts are generally issued against smaller payments, received by cash or cheque. Once again, there is no standard format. Think of a simple receipt issued when you buy something at a craft fair; or the till receipts issued by a larger retailer or petrol station. There is a world of difference between the levels of detail in the two. However, as a minimum, they should show:

- The date;

- Seller's name and customer's name;

- Description of the goods or services;

- Amount paid;

- The VAT number, if the seller is VAT registered.

Invoices and receipts are ways of issuing documents to your customers; but, as mentioned earlier, some customers will issue documentation to you, in the form of payment statements. So, it's likely you will end up with a complete mix of different types of income record.

At some point, all the documentation needs to be collated in order to calculate total income. You can give this to the accountant to do for you at the end of the year, which is effective but costly. You can give it to a book-keeper to do, either monthly or at the end of the year; again, this is effective and less costly than an accountant, but still means paying out money. Or you can do it yourself, either weekly, monthly or at the end of the year. This option may be effective, depending on your ability with numbers, and is the least costly in terms of actual expenditure, but it is costly in terms of your time.

There really is no right answer on this one. It depends on individual circumstances, resources and preferences. However, let's assume you decide to do it yourself on a monthly basis. The benefits are that the task is smaller, and your memory will be fresher. Basically, all you're doing is listing the sources of income in one place. Let's look at what that might look like for the three types of financial system.

12.5 Paper-based Records

A simple cash book with appropriate layout can be bought from any stationers. An A4 hard-backed notebook will do the job just as well, but the columns will have to be drawn in. Start each month on a new page. List the income-generating transactions in date order and put a total at the bottom.

Using this system monthly means that at the end of the year, there will be just twelve figures to collate to identify total income.

12.6 Spreadsheets

Use one workbook for all the accounts but use a separate worksheet for each type of transaction (income, expenditure etc.). List the income-generating transactions in date order and use the software to calculate a total at the bottom.

12.7 Commercial software

Each transaction will need to be converted to an invoice to enter it into the system. However, these invoices do not necessarily have to be issued to the customer. For example, PLR and ALCS do not need an invoice as they generate the appropriate documentation themselves. If there are a lot of small cash transactions, it can be time-consuming and unnecessary to issue an invoice for each one. My solution was to list all the books sold, and the prices, on a single invoice issued to myself, then accounted against the cash receipts.

12.8 Conclusion

This chapter deals with recording income. Some of that income will be taxable, some may not be. No distinction is made here between the two and there is no consideration of tax implications. At this point, we are only looking at what records you need to keep. What you do with them later is a whole different subject.

12.9 Worked Example

On page 144, you can see Anthea Rosewood's checklist for recording her various income streams.

Anthea R: Checklist for Recording Income

Income Stream	Document Types
Books sold face to face: No	Not applicable
Books sold online: No	Not applicable
Articles/short stories sold: Yes	Invoices raised on delivery Remittance notes from publishers Bank statements
Competition prizes: Yes	Notification and remittance notes from organisers Bank statements
Fees for running courses/workshops: Yes	Booking forms/invoices Cash book receipts Bank statements
Advance payments: No	Not applicable
PLR payments: No	Not applicable
ALCS payments: Yes	Notification and VAT receipts (if applicable) from organisers
Talks to membership groups	Email correspondence Cash receipts Bank statements

Figure 10 Checklist for Recording Income

12.10 References

Public Lending Rights (PLR) is a legal right of authors to receive payment from government in the UK or Ireland each time their books are borrowed from public libraries: www.bl.uk/plr. (There are equivalent systems operating in many countries but not, currently, in the US.)

Author Licensing and Collection Service (ALCS) is an organisation in the UK that collects on behalf of authors payments associated with secondary uses such as when schools photocopy pages from books: www.alcs.co.uk

13. Recording Expenditure

13.1 Introduction

Having looked at how to keep records of income; we're going to look now at recording your expenditure. Then you've got the two sides of the equation: you need to know what money came in (your income) and what money went out (your costs or expenditure). The difference between the two is your profit or loss. If your income is greater than your expenditure, you have made a profit. However, if your expenditure is greater than your income, you have made a loss. Let's start by considering where your costs might come from.

13.2 Types of Expenditure

As a writer, your expenditure can go in lots of different directions. Here are a few I thought of and there will be others you can list too:

- The cost of printing your books, if you publish independently. There is the cost of the physical books which might be minimal if you use a Print on Demand service but could be significant if you decide to have copies produced by a local printer. Additionally, there are costs associated with cover design, services of an editor and/or proofreader; the purchase of a block of ISBN numbers and so on;

- The purchase of books or magazines relating to your business and bought for the purposes of research;

- Competition entry fees;

- Train fares or mileage for travelling to courses or workshops, whether as the teacher or as a student;

- Attendance fees for courses, workshops or conferences;

- The money you pay yourself (whether that's a PAYE-managed salary within a limited company or personal drawings if you are self-employed or in a partnership);

- Taxes and insurance premiums;

- Bank charges and accounting/bookkeeping fees;

- The facility costs of running an office (and as a business owner, you do have an office, whether it's part of a serviced building, the back bedroom, or a corner of the kitchen table); however, this is another area where professional advice might be required, since there could be tax, insurance, mortgage etc. implications to designating part of your home as a business property;

- The day-to-day costs of running an office: paper for the printer; postage for sending out copies of your books, competition entries or submissions to agents; charges for your website; fee for renewing your antivirus software and so on;

- Capital purchases such as your laptop, printer, desk and filing cabinet; although for profit and loss purposes, these costs may need to be kept separate from your operational costs.

Many of these payments will be made by cheque, online transfer or credit card and will be accompanied by an invoice or a receipt from the seller, so there is an immediate paper trail. Others will tend to be cash payments, especially if it's for a small amount. All businesses should be able to provide a receipt on request; you need to get into the habit of always asking for one, even when it's just a short taxi ride from the station to a conference location, or a quick sandwich grabbed during the lunch break on a course.

13.3 Invoices and Receipts

We looked at invoices and receipts in the previous chapter. The only difference between income and expenditure is that in the first, you issue the documents, whereas in the second, the documents are issued to you. The documents themselves will be the same. And remember they will range from a formal invoice from a printer to a scrappy till receipt from a coffee bar. So once again, when it comes to sorting out total expenditure for the business, you will be faced with a complete mix of types of record.

As with income, all the bits of paper need to be collated to calculate total expenditure. It is also useful at this stage to group expenses together under different headings: direct expenses; wages; office expenses; professional fees etc. Your options for dealing with this task were spelled out last time, but bear repeating: you can give the job to the accountant to do for you at the end of the year, which is effective but costly. You can give it to a bookkeeper, either monthly or at the end of the year; again, this is effective and less costly than an accountant, but still means paying out money. Or you can do it yourself, either weekly, monthly or at the end of the year. This option may be effective, depending on your abilities with numbers, and is the least costly in terms of actual expenditure, but it is costly in terms of your time.

Once again, I'm going to assume you decide to do it yourself on a monthly basis, while the task is smaller, and your memory is fresher. You will be listing all items of expenditure in one place. Let's look at what that might look like for the three types of financial system.

13.4 Paper-based Records

A simple cash book with appropriate layout can be bought from any stationers. An A4 hard-backed notebook will do the job just as well, but the columns will have to be drawn in. Start each month on a new page. List the expense items in date order (which helps when reconciling the bank statement) and put a total at the bottom. If you are grouping expenses at this stage, have a separate column for each category of expense and total each column separately as well. Although, in theory, you can use the same page as the income record, it's probably simpler and neater to use a different book, or a different section of the same book.

Using this system on a monthly basis means that at the end of the year, there will be just twelve figures **per category of expenditure** to collate in order to identify total expenditure.

13.5 Spreadsheets

Use one workbook for all the accounts but use a separate worksheet for each type of transaction (income, expenditure etc). List the expenses in date order and use the software to calculate a total at the bottom. As above, use separate columns for different categories of expense.

13.6 Commercial software

Each transaction will need to be converted to an expense payment to enter it into the system. If the supplier has issued an invoice, this needs to be entered and then the payment is accounted against it. If there are a lot of small cash transactions, it can be time-consuming and unnecessary to enter each one separately. My solution was to pull these all together monthly as a single invoice, itemised line by line within the document. The software has the provision for allocating a category to each expense and the facility for producing reports on each category as required.

For non-receipted expenses, such as mileage, it's important to keep a written record. Every year I promise myself I will put a book in the glove-compartment and record every journey at the time it occurs; and every year the system collapses quickly or never gets started. Luckily, I keep a detailed appointment diary and have a reasonably good memory. At the end of each year, I list all my journeys and calculate the mileage using *Bing Maps,* but it takes me ages. Doing it monthly (or better still, journey by journey) would be a much more effective approach. So maybe next year...

13.7 Conclusion

This chapter is about recording expenditure. Some of that expenditure will be tax-deductible, some may not be. No distinction is made here between the two. At this point, we are only looking at what records you need to keep. What you do with them later is a whole different subject.

13.8 Worked Example

On page 156, you can see Anthea Rosewood's checklist for recording her different types of expenditure.

Anthea R: Checklist for Recording Expenditure

Expenditure	Document Type	Cost Type
Books and/or magazines purchased for training purposes of researching the market	Till receipts Receipts for online purchases	Indirect
Competition entry fess	Receipts from organisers Bank statements	Direct
Fares or mileage for travelling to courses or workshops as a student	Receipts and train tickets Mileage record book	Indirect
Attendance fees and expenses for training courses, workshops and conferences	Invoices and/or receipts from organisers Bank statements	Indirect
Fares or mileage for travelling to courses or workshops as a tutor or talks as presenter	Receipts and train tickets Mileage record book	Direct
Materials produced for students at workshops or training courses	Invoices and/or receipts from suppliers Bank statements	Direct
Venue costs associated with running workshops or training courses	Invoices and/or receipts from suppliers Bank statements	Direct
Salary or drawings	Bank statements	Indirect
Insurance premiums	Invoices and/or receipts from insurers Bank statements	Indirect
Office costs: equipment, stationery, telephone, internet, software etc	Invoices and/or receipts from suppliers Bank statements	Indirect

Figure 11 Checklist for Recording Expenditure

14. Accounting Statements

14.1 Introduction

In the past two chapters, we've looked at what records you need to keep in your small business; records both of income and of expenditure. Now we're going to start looking at why you need to keep those records and what you need to do with the data you collect.

There are two main reasons for keeping financial records. Firstly, It's a legal requirement. The law says if you earn money, you must pay tax. I know that's a very broad statement and there are all sorts of things to consider, such as whether an income stream is tax-free; or whether your earnings exceed your tax allowance level; but in general terms, if you earn, you pay tax. And yes, before you ask, that *does* apply even if it's "only a hobby". Although why you would be thinking about hobbies when you're supposed to be running a business, I have no idea.

Incidentally, although I am primarily writing about systems in the UK and the US, I think I'm safe in saying the rule "if you earn, you pay tax" applies in most other countries as well.

Financial records need to be kept for varying lengths of time, depending on your location and business structure and professional advice should be sought on your own requirements. But broadly speaking, seven years is the length of time that most people adopt.

But frankly, there's a much more important reason why you keep financial records: you need to know whether your business is successful or not. Remember the quote from Mr Micawber:

Annual income twenty pounds, annual expenditure nineteen pounds nineteen six, result happiness. Annual income twenty pounds, annual expenditure twenty pounds nought and six, result misery.

(David Copperfield by Charles Dickens).

Now, I'm not actually saying profitability is the only measure of success; but you're running a business here. You need to know whether you've made a profit or not; whether your cashflow is going to be sufficient to pay the mortgage next month and so on. As always, you should try to keep the systems as simple as possible. They should be effective, tell you what you need to know, with as little effort as possible, leaving you to concentrate on what you really want to be doing: writing.

There are three main accounting statements. I'm going to introduce all three in this chapter, then go on to talk about the two key ones in more detail. The statements are: profit and loss; balance sheet; and cashflow.

14.2 Profit and Loss

The profit and loss (P&L) statement is an historical picture of how the business has performed over a given period.

The P&L statement is usually calculated annually; it will certainly form part of your closing accounts. However, it may also be useful to monitor it monthly. If you are going to do that, it's certainly easier to do with a commercial accounts software package.

14.3 Balance Sheet

The balance sheet provides a snapshot in time; what is the business worth today? It compares the total assets (what you own in terms of equipment; money in the bank; stock waiting to be sold; and money owed to you) with the total liabilities (what you owe in long-term or short-term debts) and looks at how the business is funded. This statement is more appropriate to limited companies and only works with businesses using the accrual accounting method. It is not a mandatory requirement for self-employment/sole proprietorship or for partnerships. It can be calculated manually but is much easier to prepare at the press of a button via a software package. I'm not going to cover balance sheets in any more detail than this.

14.4 Cashflow Statement

This is arguably the most important statement for any business. It's a forward-looking document, used to plan the flow of money over time. It is particularly important if you are going to incur high expenses (for example, if you are independently-publishing a print book) or if there will be a delay before receiving payments.

In most businesses, there is a time-lag between incurring expenditure and bringing in income. Even cash businesses like shops often pay upfront for their stock, but only get income in return when the stock is sold. As a writer, you may be lucky enough to have an advance against a commissioned book (although that's becoming rarer these days) but even that will be a relatively small amount of income. If you must wait for publication, for sales to grow and for the first royalty statement to be issued (which can be six or twelve months after publication), your investment (in time, in electricity, in printing costs and so on) will occur quite a bit in advance of the expected income. You need to know if your cashflow is likely to be negative (more going out than coming in) so you can plan your funding appropriately. This is particularly important in a start-up business and applies equally whatever business structure you have chosen. We will look at cashflow in more detail in a later chapter.

14.5 Conclusion

There are two reasons for keeping financial records: not only are they are a legal requirement, but they also provide important information about the success or otherwise of your business *from a financial point of view.*

There are three main accounting statements, two of which are applicable to all businesses, while the third is only applicable to those employing the accrual accounting methodology.

15. Profit and Loss

15.1 Introduction

The profit and loss (P&L) statement may also be known as the **income and expenses statement** or the **statement of financial results** or the **statement of operations** or simply the **income statement**. As I said in the previous chapter, it provides an historical picture of how your business has performed over a given period. It's calculated annually, at the end of a financial year, but may also be calculated monthly if you wish to have more detailed knowledge of how you're doing.

The financial year is not necessarily the same as the calendar year (1st January to 31st December), although in some countries, it is exactly that. In the UK and the US, a limited company or corporation may use any year end date they wish, but it is common to use the same date as the government's Financial Year, which is 31st March in the UK and 30th September in the US. Whichever year end you pick, you must still fit in with the HMRC or IRS timetables for tax returns and payments in the UK or the US respectively.

If you are self-employed or in a partnership in the UK, your year end will usually be 5th April, in line with the individual tax year which starts on 6th April. In the US, the general rule is that the tax year is the same as the calendar year, unless permission is obtained to vary the date.

All decisions of this nature can have tax implications for your business. Always remember the mantra 'keep it simple'. And take professional advice before doing anything.

If you do want monthly statements, then you are probably at the point where a computerised system is appropriate. It's not a necessary part of running a business to know how to construct financial statements, but it is essential that you know how to interpret these statements and understand what they are telling you.

In an earlier chapter, we've already looked at the P&L equation:

Income minus costs equals profit/loss

Now we're going to look at this in a little more detail and cover five lines on the statement instead of the three quoted above.

15.2 Total Income

Total income is also sometimes called **Turnover, Revenue** or **Sales.** As the term suggests, it is a measure of the total amount of business you've done in the year. However, it will vary depending on which method of accounting is employed. It's more than likely that not all the money has been received yet, especially for any invoices raised in the last month. Under the accrual accounting method, all invoices are counted towards income, even if they are still outstanding. Under the cash accounting method, only income that has been received is counted.

15.3 Direct Expenses

Direct expenses are also sometimes called **Variable Costs** since they vary with the level of business or the **Cost of Goods Sold**. This is the expenditure incurred directly in doing the business measured above. It's the cost of printing your book, although if you are using accrual accounting, you can only include the cost of copies that have been sold; the postage for distribution of specific copies of your book; the travel costs incurred in presenting a training course or a paid-for appearance. You should ask yourself the question: would those costs have been incurred if that piece of work had not been carried out? If the answer is 'no', then those are direct expenses. Under the accrual accounting method, all bills are counted towards expenditure, even if they are still outstanding.

Under the cash accounting method, only bills that have been paid are counted.

15.4 Gross Profit

When direct expenses are deducted from total income, the resulting figure is called **Gross Profit, Margin or Gross Margin**. In traditional businesses like manufacturing, it is a measure of how efficiently labour and materials are utilised. In your writing business, you probably don't incur labour costs unless you sub-contract out a specific piece of work, so it's a measure of how efficiently you use the materials and other resources that go into generation of your income.

There is no right answer to the question: what is a good percentage gross profit? It varies with circumstances and the type of business. However, I would suggest it should always be a positive number. In other words, you should always generate a gross profit, no matter how small, in your business. Otherwise, you might just as well set fire to your money or (preferably) give it away. There may be times when you choose to sell your goods or services at cost (for example if you speak at an event for expenses only) or even make a loss (for example by donating copies of your books for a raffle) but that's not a sustainable business model in the long-term.

15.5 Indirect Expenses

Indirect expenses are sometimes called **Fixed Costs** or **Overheads** or **Operating Expenses** since they are independent of the level of business. There are all sorts of other expenses you incur while running your business, but which cannot be associated directly with any one income stream. For example, the cost of running your office, whether it is part of a serviced building or your back bedroom; marketing costs (business cards, book marks, general adverts); internet and phone charges; and most important of all, what you pay yourself. You should ask yourself the question: would those costs have been incurred even if no work had been carried out? If the answer to this question is 'yes', then you're looking at an indirect cost. Under the accrual accounting method, all bills are counted towards expenditure, even if they are still outstanding. Under the cash accounting method, only bills that have been paid are counted.

15.6 Net Profit

When the indirect expenses are subtracted from the gross profit, the resulting figure is called net profit. Mathematically, the same figure is obtained by subtracting total costs (direct and indirect) from total income. So net profit, which is sometimes referred to as the **Bottom Line**, is a measure of the overall success of the business *in financial terms* (I fully accept there are other ways of measuring success). In formal company accounts, net profit is further subdivided into net profit before tax and net profit after tax. I'm not going to go into tax, as it's a highly complex area, apart from making the point that in the same way that not all income will be taxable, not all expenses will be tax-deductible. This is an area where I believe it pays to take expert advice.

Unlike gross profit, it is very likely that in the early years of a business, net profit will be a negative figure (more correctly called **net loss**) and so long as you have funding available to cover the shortfall, that's perfectly acceptable. And that's where cashflow comes in. We'll talk about that in the next chapter.

15.7 Conclusion

The P&L statement is an important measure of the success of your business, *from a financial point of view.* It's prepared at the year end but may also be compiled monthly for a more detailed examination of your performance. It's made up of the difference between the income generated by the business and the costs, both direct and indirect, expended during the same time period

15.8 Worked Example

On page 171, you can see Anthea Rosewood's profit and loss statement for year 1, assuming her Business Plan income targets have been achieved.

Anthea Rosewood Profit and Loss Statement

Income		
	Short story sales	£5,400
	ALCS payment	£150
	Letters and shorts in magazines	£300
	Competition wins	£1250
	Talks to membership groups	£600
	Workshops delivered	£560
	Courses delivered	£1600
Total Income		£9860
Direct Costs		
	Short story submissions	£72
	Letters and shorts submissions	£120
	Competition fees	£250
	Mileage for delivering talks	£216
	Venue and materials for workshops	£210
	Venue and materials for courses	£600
Total Direct Costs		£1276
Gross profit (Total Income minus Total Direct Costs)		£8584
Indirect Costs		
	Marketing costs	£1200
	Administration costs	£1200
Total Indirect Costs		£2400
Net profit before tax (Gross Profit minus Total Indirect Costs)		£6184

Figure 12 Profit and Loss Statement

16. Cashflow Planning

16.1 Introduction

Like the P&L and the balance sheet, cashflow can be looked at historically. A cashflow statement is used to show how changes in the balance sheet have occurred over the past year. However, I believe it is much more important as a planning tool and it is this aspect I'm going to focus on. For those of you who have read the first section of this book, *Business Start-Up*, there will be an element of revision in this chapter, as we have already talked about cashflow as part of the initial planning process.

Cashflow is used to examine the expected flow of money over a given period, which may be years, but will certainly be months. It allows you to identify your cash requirements, to spot any periods when you can expect a deficit and then to plan the funding of that deficit.

It is not part of the record-keeping needed to work out how much you owe the tax man or *vice versa*, so a cashflow plan is not a statutory requirement. However, I would suggest it's one of the most important tools in your box. It is particularly critical if you are likely to incur high expenses (which may be the case when you are starting a business) or if there is expected to be a time lag before payments will be received. This sort of time lag is certainly one that most writers will recognise.

A cashflow plan is an easy document to prepare and is best done either on paper, although this means you will have to do the sums in your head, or in a spreadsheet. It can also be done within a computerised accounting package, but I'm not sure it's worth the bother. Personally, I would opt for the spreadsheet every time. Set it up with a column for each month. Start with a year and when that's done, you can decide whether you need to carry it forward for a second year or more. The plan can be based on actual or projected figures and will often be a mixture of both. You often *know* what your expenses are going to be, while you merely have expectations on levels and timing of income.

16.2 Income

You start by brainstorming all the income streams you're hoping to tap during the next year; together with the expected amounts and **mostly importantly** the timing of receipt. This is not about raising invoices; you can't pay a bill with an invoice. This is about getting money into the bank. And it's also about knowing and understanding the payment systems operated by your various customers.

Let's take an example:

Suppose you are commissioned to write a series of monthly articles for a writing magazine and you are offered a fixed fee per article. The series will run from July through to December. The delivery date for the first article is April and then monthly thereafter. You will raise your invoices monthly from April onwards. There are a couple of possibilities for payment:

- The magazine may pay within a set period of invoice date; this could be 30 days, it could be 60 days, it could even be 90 days. The key thing is to know what to expect. Let's assume they pay within 30 days of invoice date. The first money should be paid at the end of May and therefore would be available to deal with June's bills.

- The magazine may pay at the end of the month of publication. In this case, the first money would be paid at the end of July and would be available for August's bills.

So, there's a possibility that work carried out in April will not provide any positive cashflow until August. Of course, with a monthly contract, you know there will be money coming in each month from then on, for as long as the contract exists and for the three or four months' time lag thereafter.

If you think about other income sources, there is often a delay associated with payment. For example, money from sales of ebooks may be delayed until a threshold amount of sales has been made; and secondly according to payment policy. Amazon has recently abolished thresholds, but payment is not made until 60 days following the end of the calendar month in which sales were made. Some other ebook platforms still operate thresholds. So, there could be quite a time lag to build in.

Of course, some income can be obtained up front: cash from books sold direct to the reader; fees paid by students on writing courses or seminars; advances from publishers on commissioned books are three examples I can think of. On the other hand, the royalties paid by publishers on traditionally published books can be delayed by months, if not years.

Once you've identified all likely income streams and the timing of expected payments, each stream is listed as a separate row on the spreadsheet and the income payments listed in the appropriate column. You can then calculate your expected income *by month* over the chosen period.

Next, we'll look at expenditure planning (depressingly easier to do than income planning) and dealing with cashflow deficits.

16.3 Expenditure

With expenditure, there tends to be more certainty, especially with regard to fixed costs (the costs you incur whether or not you have any work). For example, you know what rent or rates you're going to pay. You know what your utility bills are going to be. You know how much you're paying for your phone. All of these tend to be regular payments that can be entered in the monthly columns.

Of course, if you're working from home and charging a proportion of the household costs to the business, you can choose to do this annually rather than monthly—or even to waive the charge altogether until the business is established. But if you do this, you must remember you're giving yourself a false picture when assessing how successful you have been.

The variable costs (those associated with a specific piece of work) are a little more difficult but for each income figure you enter, you should be able to estimate the related costs. These need to be entered at the time they are incurred (or at least paid for) which will often be before the income arrives.

To finish the statement, you need an opening balance for the beginning of the year and a carried forward figure at the end of each period (month). Remember you do not start each month afresh. If you have a deficit at the end of one month, that is the opening balance at the start of the next month.

As the months go by, replace estimated figures with actual ones; this will help to keep your cashflow planning up to date.

OK, I think it's now time for some examples. Remember, the only purpose of these examples is to illustrate the points, so please don't get hung up on whether the individual numbers make sense or not.

16.4 Worked Example 1

In this example, which is shown on page 183, imagine you have four different income streams:

- six articles paid monthly between August and January;

- Amazon sales which come in bimonthly from October onwards;

- direct sales to the public which vary depending on events per month;

- and fees for running writing courses every two months.

Your income varies between £20 and £370 per month.

For expenditure, you have the following items:

- a regular monthly contract for phone and internet;

- mileage costs and printing costs associated with the course, the former occurring in the same month and the latter a month earlier in each case;

- and a regular 'drawing' to cover personal expenses. Whether this is a salary you are paid as an employee of a limited company/corporation, or whether it is a drawing you make as a sole trader is irrelevant here. This is the money you need to live.

Your total expenditure is fairly fixed at between £550 and £580 per month (and again, remember, these are examples only, not real figures).

You have started the year with an opening balance, i.e. funding, of £4,000. At the end of the year, your closing balance is zero. This means you are projecting a loss of £4,000 during the year. But remember, we're talking here about cashflow. What this tells us is that if you start with £4,000, you will have enough cash to last the year but will need to sort out more funding, raise income, or reduce expenditure at the beginning of the next financial year.

16.5 Worked Example 2

Now, let's suppose you don't have a £4,000 pot to start the year off. What happens if you only have £3,000? You can see this example on page 184.

In this case, your cashflow goes negative in September and you need more funding at that point, but you know you can start with a smaller pot and keep the business running for several months.

If you have your cashflow set up in a spreadsheet, as I've shown here, it's very easy to play the 'what if' game by changing some of the figures and seeing what the effect is on the bottom line. For example, try pushing up the income or reducing the expenditure to see what happens. This is also useful for crystallising exactly what you need to do to make the business a success in financial terms. But remember to keep your scenarios realistic. Overly optimistic cashflow plans can lead to trouble.

	A	M	J	J	A	S	O	N	D	J	F	M
Opening Balance	4000	3440	3160	2630	2430	1970	1790	1380	1380	970	790	280
Income												
Articles					100	100	100	100	100	100		
Amazon Sales							50		50		50	
Direct Book Sales	20	20	50	100	20	20	20	200	20	20	20	20
Course Fees		250		250		250		250		250		250
Total Income	20	270	50	350	120	370	170	550	170	370	70	270
Expenditure												
Phone/Internet	30	30	30	30	30	30	30	30	30	30	30	30
Mileage		20		20		20		20		20		20
Printing costs (courses)	50		50		50	50	50		50		50	
Personal expenses	500	500	500	500	500	500	500	500	500	500	500	500
Total Expenditure	580	550	580	550	580	550	580	550	580	550	580	550
Closing Balance	3440	3160	2630	2430	1970	1790	1380	1380	970	790	280	0

Figure 13 Cashflow Planning Example 1

	A	M	J	J	A	S	O	N	D	J	F	M
Opening Balance	3000	2440	2160	1630	1430	970	790	380	380	-30	-210	-720
Income												
Articles					100	100	100	100	100	100		
Amazon Sales	20		50				50		50		50	20
Direct Book Sales		20		100	20	20	20	200	20	20	20	
Course Fees		250		250		250		250		250		250
Total Income	20	270	50	350	120	370	170	550	170	370	70	270
Expenditure												
Phone/Internet	30	30	30	30	30	30	30	30	30	30	30	30
Mileage		20		20		20		20		20		20
Printing costs (courses)	50		50		50		50		50		50	
Personal expenses	500	500	500	500	500	500	500	500	500	500	500	500
Total Expenditure	580	550	580	550	580	550	580	550	580	550	580	550
Closing Balance	2440	2160	1630	1430	970	790	380	380	-30	-210	-720	-1000

Figure 14 Cashflow Planning Example 2

16.6 Conclusion

While cashflow planning is not one of the activities required for tax calculation, it is a critical part of managing your finances and therefore your business. A simple spreadsheet is a perfectly adequate method for setting up a plan and can be used to review 'what if' scenarios. The plan should be set up with at least monthly columns and should extend for at least a year. The data included will be a mixture of accurate figures, often associated with fixed costs, and estimates, especially for income and variable costs.

17. Risk Management

17.1 Introduction

This final chapter is a little different from the previous ones as it doesn't deal with a formal finance system. However, it's an important area that shouldn't be forgotten. All businesses are subject to risk and your business as a writer is no exception. These days, risk management has become a huge topic: the subject of whole books; the purpose of entire corporate departments; and the originator of reams of documents and forms. However, that's not the approach we're going to take here. You're just going to think for a while about possible risks and how you would deal with them. Once you've done that, you can forget all about it. If the risks never materialise, you've lost maybe an hour or so of your time. If the worst does happen, you'll know what to do and will be less fazed by the problems, whatever they may be.

Risk management is a three-part process. Whatever your business:

- risks have to be identified;

- risks have to be assessed;

- and risks have to be managed.

In your writing business, they might include: risks of under-resourcing; health and safety risks; or credit risks.

If you work on your own, and you get sick or you have too many projects to complete—although that could be considered a nice problem to deal with—you could lose customers through being unable to work. What about the situation where two important book fairs are scheduled for the same day? You can't split yourself into two. These are risks of under-resourcing.

There is the risk you might be injured on a customer's property or a customer might be injured on your property. These are health and safety risks.

There is the risk your customer might default on payment. This is a credit risk.

As a business owner, you need a risk management process for two reasons. Firstly you think about potential risks in advance and put contingency plans in place, allowing you to get on with business, without worrying about things going wrong. And secondly, it may be a regulatory requirement, especially health and safety risk assessment, and government or local officials may wish to see evidence of your risk assessment process.

17.2 Risk Management Process

With so many different types of risks to consider, it's not necessary to address each one in a different way. What is required is a simple approach where risk management becomes part of 'the way things are done around here'. You have a generic risk assessment process, flexible enough to fit all circumstances and a simple risk assessment form covering the four stages of the process. And when I say simple, I'm thinking of a blank piece of paper on which you write down your thoughts and conclusions; it really is that simple.

17.3 Stage 1: Checking for Hazards

A hazard is a reality—something already existing. Cables stretched across the floor; a dangerous chemical used as part of the job, and yes, I know the most dangerous chemical a writer works with is probably Tipp-Ex (and for the benefit of my younger readers, that's liquid correction fluid) but bear with me; it's just an example; or a customer who's having financial difficulties. Each of these is a hazard you might come across.

17.4 Stage 2: Identifying Risks

A risk is something that might happen. Someone might fall over the cables; chemicals might splash in someone's eye; the customer might go bust before paying your bill. They are possibilities, not certainties.

17.5 Stage 3: Probability and Severity

Probability deals with how likely something is to happen. If the cable is at the front of the office where people are continually walking, or across the aisle at a busy book fair, the probability of someone falling over it is greater than if it's in a back office or behind a stall where people rarely go.

Severity deals with how bad the consequences would be if a risk becomes a reality. If someone gets a paper cut from one of your books, the severity is low, although paper cuts do sting, don't they? On the other hand, if chemicals splash in someone's eyes, it could blind them or at least stop them working for a time, so the severity is much higher.

Probability and severity are considered separately since they are independent of each other. For example, the severity of chemicals splashing in someone's eyes is high, but the probability is much lower in your writing business than in a chemical factory, and now you see why I needed that example in my list. If you were running the factory, you would need to install eye bath stations, or maybe even showers, against the risk of chemical burns. In your writing business, that's not a measure you're likely to have to take. Having said that, it's important to make sure the top is tight on the Tipp-Ex bottle before giving it a good shake.

A simple method for comparing and classifying individual risks is to use a pseudo-quantitative approach to assessment. In each case, probability is scored as 1 (low), 2 (medium) or 3 (high) and severity is scored as 1 (minor), 2 (medium) or 3 (very severe). Then the two scores are multiplied together to give a ranking score of 1 to 9, where the higher the number, the greater the overall risk.

17.6 Stage 4: Dealing With Risks

Once you know the size of the potential problems, you can decide what to do about them. You might decide the cable should be rerouted or a sign put up to warn people to be careful; that's avoidance of risk. You would ensure anyone working with the chemical wears eye protection; that's elimination of risk. You might take out insurance against defaulting customers or insist on payment in advance; that's mitigation of risk.

17.7 Your Own Risks

If you think back to the previous chapter, cashflow planning could be a risk management process. Is there a risk you might run out of cash at some point in the future and if so, is there a strategy in place to overcome the problem? So, this isn't really an alien concept at all.

However, as a writer, one of the greatest risks you have relates to storage of your files. After all, those files contain your work in progress, your finished products, your orders, and your financial records; pretty much everything you need to run your business. So, let's do a quick risk assessment.

- A **hazard** could be that you store all the files relating to your business on one single computer or laptop. That would be a fact.

- A **risk** would be that the computer suffers a fatal breakdown and all your files become corrupted or lost. That would be a possibility.

- The **probability** would depend on factors such as the age of the computer, the storage method you're using, the nature of the computer problem and just how susceptible you are to Sod's Law.

- The **severity** of the problem is such that I can feel you shuddering from here!

So how do you manage this very real risk to your business as a writer? It's highly unlikely you can eliminate the risk altogether. Computers do break down, often at the most inconvenient time. I lost my machine some years ago, just a week before I was due to deliver a manuscript to my publisher. It was at the time when we were migrating from Word 2003 to Word 2007; the whole look of the thing changed, and I needed to learn how to use the new software while finishing the final edits. It was not a good week!

So, if you can't eliminate, you must mitigate or avoid the effects of the risk. That might be by using an external drive that can be removed from the machine and stored elsewhere; by making multiple back-ups regularly; or by using a cloud-based storage system like Drop Box. Once you have these systems in place, and you know they are working well, you can forget about them until or unless the worst happens. And when it does, it will be a mere inconvenience, rather than a disaster.

17.8 Conclusion

Risk management doesn't have to be daunting. All it takes is a bit of thought, a generic step-wise process and a simple risk assessment form. It's worth spending an hour thinking through the risks in your business and planning what you would do if a risk became a reality. Then you can put it to one side and get on with what you really want to do: your writing.

17.9 Worked Example

On page 197, you can see the Risk Assessment carried out by Anthea Rosewood when she was planning to set up her own business.

Risk Assessment

Hazard	Risk	Probability (1)	Severity (2)	Risk Score	Prevention/Mitigation
Storage of files on laptop computer	Loss of data through theft or damage	2	3	6	Move to use of Drop Box for regular storage of files Use of detachable hard drive for weekly back-ups.
Use of internet for correspondence and research	Subject to hacking or other malicious intervention	3	3	9	Purchase of annual subscription to proprietary anti-virus software (not a freebie)
Use of outside venues for workshops and courses	Venue not available when required	2	3	6	Make provisional bookings up to 12 months in advance, with agreed cancellation policy if necessary.
	Member of public injured while taking part in course or workshop	1	2-3	2-3	Carry out risk assessment as preparation for any event in an outside venue. Make sure appropriate insurance is in place.
Working as a single, self-employed person	Taken ill and unable to work	1	3	3	Investigate the possibility of insurance to cover this eventuality

Notes

1 = low; 2 = medium; 3 = high

2 = minor; 2 = medium; 3 = severe

Figure 15 Risk Assessment

197

Section 3: Improving Effectiveness

18. Becoming More Effective

18.1 Introduction

There are only three things one needs to do to succeed in business:

- Get the work;

- Do the work;

- Get paid for the work.

In the first two sections of this book, we focused mainly on the first and third items on that list.

In this section, we're going to concentrate on the middle part, and arguably the most difficult of the three: delivering the work. But we're not going to look at it from the traditional viewpoint. This book is not about improving the content of what you write. What we're going to look at instead are some of the tools available to make you a more effective writer and business owner: using your time more effectively; planning your writing projects efficiently; and applying traditional problem-solving techniques both to your business and to your writing.

18.2 Why Should You Care?

You're a writer; you're running, or getting ready to run, your own small business. You're living the dream. So why do you need to even think about doing things more effectively? Should you even care?

I would suggest you should—and you probably already do. The pace of life in the twenty-first century is faster than ever before. Communications have speeded up immeasurably. Many of us are online throughout our waking lives, reading and responding to emails, Facebook posts, Tweets and so on. Technological improvements allow us to do things we would never have dreamed of just ten or twenty years before.

And as a result, we all put far too much stress on ourselves. We want to do it all; have it all; be successful. And even when we're doing the job we love—writing—we find ourselves running to keep pace with everything we want to do. And never saying no—to anything. (Maybe that should be the next book in this series: *The Business of Writing Part 6 Learning To Say No.*)

And what happens to all those stretch targets, those impossibly long To Do lists we set ourselves? We fail. We don't manage to do everything we want to; and that hurts. It's depressing. It makes us think we're not as good as everyone else. When in fact, everyone else is probably just as stressed out and anxious as we are.

18.3 Searching For Perfection?

So, am I suggesting you should be searching for perfection? That can be really, really stressful! I should know; my birthday's in September and although the scientist in me has always been somewhat dismissive of astrology, I have to admit to being a typical Virgo. I obsess over small details, determined to get them right, and once I've committed to doing something, I keep at it, no matter how hard it gets. I also set myself impossibly difficult targets and deadlines.

Someone accused me recently of being 'totally sorted' and possibly 'too perfect'. Oh boy, has she got me wrong! Although, it does mean my acting talents are improving and my swan-like surface calm is succeeding in disguising the utter panic below the surface.

So, no, this section is definitely NOT about searching for perfection.

18.4 Being Kind To Yourself

It's about being kind to yourself. And there are all sorts of ways of doing that, of course. Taking a break; getting some exercise each day, away from your desk. Practising meditation. Working on your mindfulness. But there are plenty of other people out there writing books or recording videos on those aspects.

What we're going to look at in this book are a few ways you can use your time more effectively. There are tools for analysing what you do, so you can decide where your priorities lie. Tools for planning your writing projects so you know in advance what you need to do, and when, in order to have a better chance of finishing on time. And a few suggestions for cutting corners along the way.

There is no suggestion you need to apply all the techniques from this book. That would be impossible. The idea is to provide you with a box of tools and some thoughts about how and when you might want to use those tools. And if something works for you, then use it, adapt it as you wish. If it doesn't, then leave it and move on.

I started this chapter by saying you are living the dream. But sometimes the dream gets a little nightmarish. I want this section to help relieve the stress, push away the bad dreams, and get back to enjoying what you really want to be doing—running your own small business as a writer.

19. Project Management

19.1 Introduction

Let's start with a definition. What is a project? A project is a unique **process**, consisting of a set of co-ordinated and controlled **activities** with start and finish dates, undertaken to achieve an objective conforming to specific requirements, including constraints of **time**, **cost** and **resources.** In other words, it is a series of tasks that must be completed in order and to specific requirements, to achieve a particular objective. And a successful project is one that's completed on time, to specification and at cost.

But a writer is a creative person; you work when the muse visits you, and sometimes when she's noticeably absent. You don't have to worry about working to project plans like someone with a 'proper' jobs. Right? Wrong! Whether you're writing an article that's been commissioned for a particular edition of a magazine; a short story for a competition; or a blog posting that's due on a Monday, you work on projects most of the time. Even if you're writing your first novel, without the pressure of a contract and an agent breathing down your necks—although that could be a nice pressure to deal with—you will probably have self-imposed milestones you're working towards.

19.2 Project Realities

From my experience, there are a few things that are common to all projects:

- The start date often slips back; and the more time you have to complete the project, the more likely you are to let it slide on the basis that there's always plenty of time to catch up later;

- Resources often get side-tracked or reassigned. In your case, your main resource is usually your time, so refer to the previous point;

- Finish dates are often outside your control and set in stone (or they may even be pulled forward).

A professional project manager will divide each project into five or six stages: proposal; definition; start-up; execution; control; and close. This is because getting the project approved (in terms of scope, cost etc) is often the first stage. If you're writing a non-fiction book, which you hope to get traditionally published, you would go through all these stages since you would have to approach a publisher with a proposal and get the work commissioned before you would start writing.

However, that brings in a whole different subject. So, we're going to start with the assumption that your writing project will definitely go ahead—and thus, you will only think about what you need to do from start-up onwards.

19.3 Plan, Do and Review

In simple terms, there are really only three things to do in a project: Plan; Do; and Review (PDR). In fact, you can take this approach at all sorts of levels in the project. For example, if you write an article for a specific magazine, you will plan the article, write it (which may involve research, interviews etc) and review it for accuracy, editing etc. So that's one level of PDR.

Now, supposing your overall objective is to repurpose that article and resell it elsewhere; or to use it as part of your portfolio in looking for other work; or use it as your submission for Journalist of the Year—whatever your overall project, you can go through the same PDR exercise and your original article project will be one sub-project of the overall one.

Also, remember that your main project may well be a sub-project for someone else. If you have a contract to write a book, you can develop a project plan for the writing itself; however, for your publisher, that will just be one step in the overall process of getting the book published.

19.4 Project Planning

A project plan is useful for two purposes. Firstly, it helps to determine **in advance** what needs to be done so you can ensure you have sufficient resources, especially time, in which to do it. But, it can also be used **retrospectively** to measure what was achieved and therefore whether your project management process is successful. If it is, you have a methodology which can be reused on future projects; remember that reinventing the wheel is a time-wasting activity. On the other hand, if it has been unsuccessful in some way, you can review what you did, learn from your mistakes and adjust your planning process for future projects.

19.5 Producing Plans

Plans can be drawn up in two ways. They can be derived by working forwards from today, estimating how much time is needed for each stage and seeing where that takes you. However, this is less controlled, and you tend to be more generous with your time slots.

Alternatively, your plans can be developed by working backwards from a fixed point in the future. This is the method that has to be used if you have a deadline imposed by a customer or other external force. For example, filing a tax return is a necessary evil in your business life and there are set deadlines by which it has to be in, unless you want to face financial penalties for late delivery. Working in this way, there may well be resource constraints, and these need to be resolved.

Project plans can be produced manually, using words, pictures or mind maps. We will talk more about this very useful technique in chapter 21, but in the meantime, on page 213, you can see one of the mind maps I prepared when I was starting this project, back in September 2017.

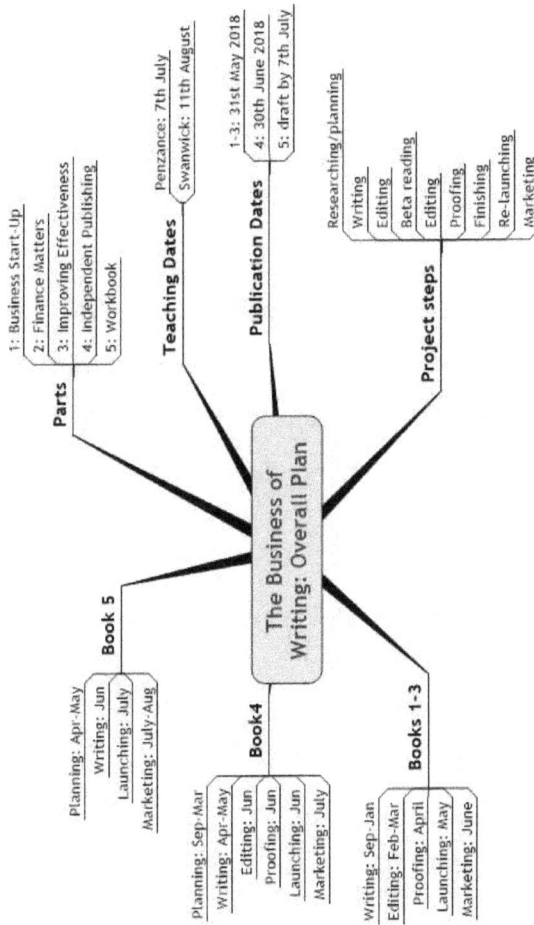

The Business of Writing: Overall Plan

Parts
1: Business Start-Up
2: Finance Matters
3: Improving Effectiveness
4: Independent Publishing
5: Workbook

Teaching Dates
Penzance: 7th July
Swanwick: 11th August

Publication Dates
1-3: 31st May 2018
4: 30th June 2018
5: draft by 7th July

Project steps
Researching/planning
Writing
Editing
Beta reading
Editing
Proofing
Finishing
Re-launching
Marketing

Book 5
Planning: Apr-May
Writing: Jun
Launching: July
Marketing: July-Aug

Book4
Planning: Sep-Mar
Writing: Apr-May
Editing: Jun
Proofing: Jun
Launching: Jun
Marketing: July

Books 1-3
Writing: Sep-Jan
Editing: Feb-Mar
Proofing: April
Launching: May
Marketing: June

Figure 16 Mind Map for Project Planning

213

Alternatively, your plan can be developed electronically. When I worked in industry, I used specialised software to plan my projects, but these days I use spreadsheets to set up simple bar charts for my planning, starting at the end and working backwards, as Worked Example 1 shows.

Before we look at some examples, I want to talk about tasks and milestones, both of which appear in a project plan. A **task** is an activity undertaken over time; it is a thing you need to do. A **milestone** is an occurrence at a single point in time; it is a tangible achievement resulting from completing a series of tasks.

19.6 Worked Example 1: Overview Plan

Let's imagine that at the beginning of March 2019, you decide to write a book about a particular historical event that took place in your home town/village in July 1920. The book is scheduled for publication to coincide with the centenary of said historical event.

I should emphasise here that the timescales for a self-published book are generally much shorter than for a traditionally published one. If you were to be commissioned to write this book, the period required for editing and proofing in particular would be much longer and hence the book would have been commissioned probably a year earlier. Reduced timescales is one of the advantages of self-publishing.

With this project, there's a clear deadline for publication: 1st July 2020. There will be no negotiation on that date; it's been set in stone for nearly 100 years. You need to work out how long you can spend on research and how long on writing. So, let's start by running through the stages of the project and working out which ones are fixed and beyond your control:

- Research; photos & maps; interview

- Drafting

- Writing

- Editing & proofing

- Copy deadline (milestone)

- Printing

- Cover design

- Pre-publicity and marketing

You're going to use a local printer who has told you to allow one month for the physical production of the books; so, the copy deadline is fixed at the end of May 2020. If you allow three months for editing and proofing, that takes you back to the end of February. So, you know you have twelve months for all the research, drafting and writing. How you plan those twelve months depends on your style of writing. Some writers can do the two activities in parallel; others need to have all their notes and research in place before they start. Personally, I'm in the latter group and would probably devote six months to research and plan to start writing at the start of September 2019.

Activity	Mar-19	Apr-19	May-19	Jun-19	Jul-19	Aug-19	Sep-19	Oct-19	Nov-19	Dec-19	Jan-20	Feb-20	Mar-20	Apr-20	May-20	Jun-20	Jul-20
Launch 01 07 20																	■
Printing (1 month)																■	
Editing and proofing (3 months)													■	■	■		
Writing (6 months)							■	■	■	■	■	■					
Research/interviews (6 months)	■	■	■	■	■	■											
Cover design (up to 15 months)	■	■	■	■	■	■	■	■	■	■	■	■	■	■	■		
Pre-launch publicity (9 months)									■	■	■	■	■	■	■	■	■

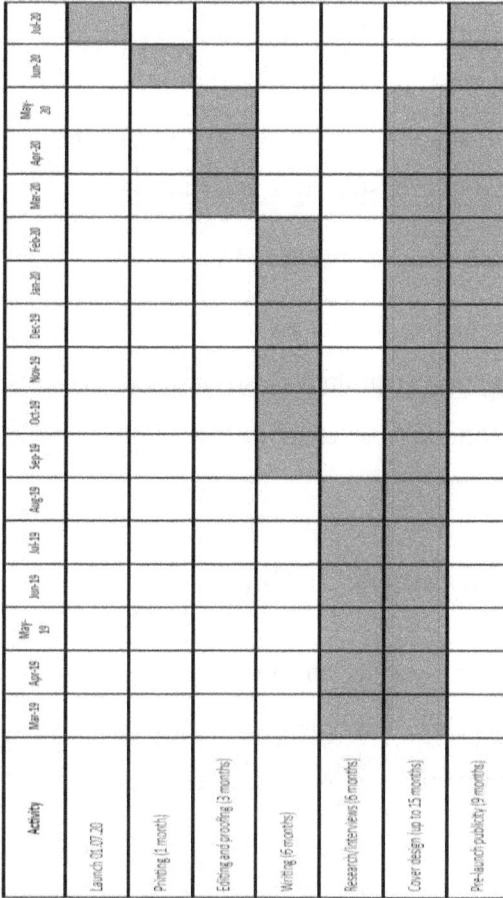

Figure 17 Bar Chart for Project Planning

Realistically, a task of six months is probably too long; it's not easy to monitor progress and it's a long time to wait before finding you are off-course. So the research stage would probably be split into desk research, interviewing, writing notes and so on; while the writing stage could be split into first draft, second draft, final draft.

The last two activities on the list are shared with other people and can be done simultaneously with the main project. You can find the bar chart for this project on page 217.

19.7 Worked Example 2: Detailed Plan

Let's have a look at planning and executing a project in more detail. We'll use a simple project like entering a short story competition as our example in this case and think back to the **Plan, Do, Review model** we discussed above.

At the **Planning** stage you need to consider **your objectives**, which are to enter a given competition. Next, you define your **measurement criteria**, otherwise you won't know whether your project has succeeded or not. These might be:

- winning a prize or getting an honorable mention;

- receiving a favourable critique from the judges;

- or simply completing the story within the correct word count and getting your entry submitted.

After all, it's your project, so you can decide on the success parameters.

Your **overall time plan** is clear: submit an entry by the closing date. However, for this to be more useful, you need to break it down into a series of **milestones**: writing the first draft; editing and polishing; giving it to beta readers/proofreaders, whether that's your writing group or a trusted friend who will give honest feedback; completion of the final version; and submission. Then to produce the **outline schedule**: you work backwards from the closing date and divide the available time appropriately. You also need to know the **user**

requirements, which in this case are the rules of the competition.

In the case of a simple project like this, there's no need for a **sign-off on the plan**, but for a more complex project (such as writing your non-fiction history book for a traditional publisher), this will probably be an iterative process with the previous stage until you and the customer are happy and ready to sign the contract (which is really a glorified project plan).

The next stage in the project is to **Do** it; in other words, to get on with the writing. You will probably find it helpful to monitor your progress against the milestones as you go along, to make sure you're keeping to the plan.

The final stage is to **Review,** and this can be considered in two ways:

- firstly, was the content okay: reviewing the writing, getting it read, proofread etc., making necessary changes and finalising the entry for submission;

- and secondly was the process okay: reviewing the project planning and management, was the split of time appropriate, was there enough time to do everything.

19.8 Just A Tool

Having discussed the use of planning as a tool for managing your projects, I'm going to finish this chapter with a word of warning. In the first example, for the project to write a history book, we saw how most of the steps were sequential and would be done in order. This is a traditional or 'waterfall' plan. It is the sort a construction company would use when building a house. The foundations would go in first; next would be the walls; and finally, they would put on the roof. Any attempt to reverse the order is likely to end in disaster.

But as a writer, you are not following a set procedure; you're working creatively. If you're writing a novel, one approach might be to map out the whole story before starting to write. Another option might be to start with an opening sentence and see where it takes you. You could write the last scene and then work back from there. Or you could write lots of scenes at random and then fit them together. I've used all these approaches at one time or another. It all depends on what you are writing and the way that suits you best.

If you have a project plan that stifles your creativity and stops you from getting the job done, it is not only a waste of time; it's counter-productive. A plan is just a tool; it's not an end in itself—although I know that might sound like heresy to some of my project management colleagues . It's important to recognise any key milestones—such as a deadline from an editor—but outside of this, you work in a way that suits you. And if that means starting at chapter six because it's a key point from which you can write in both directions—then that's what you should do.

19.9 Conclusion

Any piece of work you undertake can be considered as a project and will benefit from an element of project planning. The level to which this is carried out will depend on a number of factors including the complexity of the project, the timescales and the number of people involved in its execution. Planning can be done in a number of ways, using a variety of tools from a pencil and paper to a specialised software package. However, for many projects, especially those you are completing on your own, a spreadsheet works very well. Plans can be constructed either forwards or backwards; the latter is a more effective method, although it may be subject to tight timescales.

20. Time Management

20.1 Introduction

You now have a project plan and you know what you need to do, in which order and by when. So far, so good. But this project plan only has meaning if you carry it out.

I am lucky enough to write for a living. It's my full-time job. Which means I have at least thirty-five hours a week when I can be sitting at my laptop turning out stunning prose with which to impress my readers. Right? Wrong!

In fact, I don't know any writer who claims to have too much, or even enough, time on their hands. On the contrary, we all seem to be short of time—all the time—which gives us an excuse not to write. Firstly, we have to make time for the other writerly activities like research, editing and reading (and yes, reading is definitely part of a writer's working day). Then there are the business-related activities like writing proposals, preparing invoices, paying bills and doing the monthly accounts. There's that huge millstone that's marketing and sales (one all writers, especially indie authors, will recognise). And all this is before we even think about the personal, home-related and community-related activities on our To Do lists. Personally, if I manage to reserve twenty hours per week for new writing, I feel I'm doing well; and I suspect I'm not alone in that.

Please don't think I'm complaining. I love my job; I love my lifestyle. And I know I have it far easier than anyone who's writing while holding down a full-time job. But I wanted to illustrate the importance to all of us of time management as part of a writer's Business Skills Toolbox.

Let's consider the issue of supply and demand. You can't do anything about the supply of time on a day-to-day basis. You have the same 24 hours or 1,440 minutes per day as everybody else. You should not be considering how you can make more time; that's a physical impossibility. What you need to consider is how you can use the time you have available more effectively.

I would classify my approach to life as that of a grasshopper. I was working in an industrial setting for more than thirty years before I became a full-time writer. Simultaneously, I co-ran a small business for more than twenty years. I get involved in other activities at the drop of a hat and jump from one thing to another as they take my interest. I couldn't have done that without learning to manage my time and multi-task. Let's look at some of my tips for effective time management.

20.2 Diaries

A diary is a critical tool, recording **when** you have to do something. I use a hard copy one, A5 size or smaller, which will fit in my handbag. I've tried electronic formats, but they don't work for me. I need to be able to flick through the pages. That could be age-related, and many younger writers will probably use their phones or tablets instead. The key thing is to decide which format suits you best—and to keep it with you at all times.

A diary needs to be flexible, as priorities will change. If it's electronic, it can easily be updated. In my hard copy diary, I use pencil, NEVER pen—and I always have an eraser handy.

My Swanwick buddy, Katherine Bolton, recommends using a separate diary for writing versus the other parts of your life. That way, you can record things like competition deadlines and other writing goals all together. It's a matter of choice again. I prefer to have one main diary, as writing is so inextricably bound up with everything else, I can't separate it; but then I use a separate spreadsheet for all my competition deadlines. As I said above, the important thing is to identify what works best for each one of us—and to stick to it.

20.3 To Do lists

A To Do list is a way of reviewing **what** you have to do, and can be prepared on a daily, weekly or monthly basis; or indeed a combination of these. It works providing you remember to review it periodically and check progress. It is different from a diary; it identifies what tasks you have to do, while you use your diary to schedule blocks of time to carry out those tasks.

I prepare my monthly list in two stages. I start by drawing a mind map (see chapter 21 for more details on this great tool) with a different branch for each category of activity (writing; marketing; administration etc.). This acts as a brain dump and often helps to reduce any feelings of stress over having too much to do. You can see a part-completed one of mine on page 230.

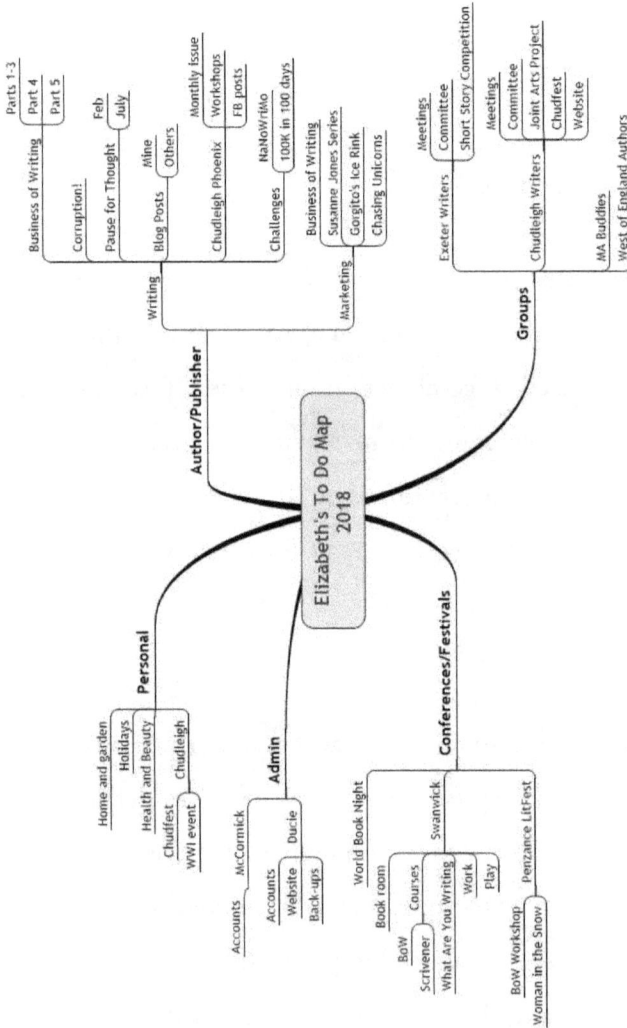

Figure 18 Mind Mapping a To Do List

Next, I list the actual tasks on a spreadsheet with due dates and priority level. Level one is a task with an absolute deadline or a firm commitment; level two tasks have more leeway on their completion date. Finally, I sort the list against due date and priority, and thus have a series of tasks for each day of the month. I always try to start the day with the tasks categorised as level one and generally manage to cross them off. Anything that's not finished one day is carried forward to the next and, if necessary, upgraded from level two to level one. You can see part of my list as of 19th May 2018 on page 232. I am up to date with the level one tasks, but some of the level two tasks, especially those relating to social media posting, have been neglected.

I would normally have all my personal activities on there as well as the business ones. The beauty of having an integrated list is I can see the whole picture in one place and make informed decisions about prioritising when I have too much to do on any one day. Which, as you can probably see, happens quite frequently!

What	By When	Priority
Set up 3 daily Instagram postings	13-May	2
Working on launch plan for BoW 1-3	14-May	1
Weekly blog post	14-May	1
Set up 3 daily postings on Instagram, Pinterest and Twitter	14-May	2
Daily Facebook and LinkedIn postings	14-May	2
Finish sending out invitations to the Literary Festival	14-May	1
Set up CP page 7	15-May	1
Set up CP pages 10-12	15-May	1
Set up CP page 14	15-May	1
Set up CP page 1	15-May	1
Write distribution email	15-May	1
Send out this month's CP	15-May	1
Prepare for 11th November meeting	15-May	1
Prepare for IAP meeting	15-May	1
Prepare for CWC committee meeting	15-May	1
Set up 3 daily postings on Instagram, Pinterest and Twitter	15-May	2
Daily Facebook and LinkedIn postings	16-May	2
Set up 3 daily postings on Instagram, Pinterest and Twitter	16-May	2
Daily Facebook and LinkedIn postings	16-May	2
Set up 3 daily postings on Instagram, Pinterest and Twitter	17-May	2
Daily Facebook and LinkedIn postings	17-May	2
Set up LitFest planning document	18-May	2
Sort out jobs and recruit volunteers for 11th July	18-May	2
Set up 3 daily postings on Instagram, Pinterest and Twitter	18-May	2
Daily Facebook and LinkedIn postings	18-May	2
CWC weekly blog post	19-May	1
Set up 3 daily postings on Instagram, Pinterest and Twitter	19-May	2
Daily Facebook and LinkedIn postings	19-May	2

Figure 19 Spreadsheet To Do List

20.4 Musts and Wants

This is linked to the priority levels in the previous section. You need to learn to distinguish between items with a deadline, which are your MUSTS and those which can be moved around or pushed back, which are your WANTS. Also, on your list of MUSTS is anything on which you're not prepared to compromise, such as supper with the family or reading those bedtime stories to the kids.

When a MUST needs to be achieved, you have to ignore all the WANTS and concentrate on just one thing. Chances are, you'll achieve it more quickly and effectively that way. When you've cleared the immediate MUSTS, you can go back to the WANTS. Personally, this is the time when I release the inner grasshopper and let her play for a while.

Before we move away from lists, I want to say just a final word of warning about list and priorities. I attended a seminar some years ago by Phil Sampson of Sampson Hall. He was talking about Leadership and Business Strategy, but one of the points he made could be applied just as easily to your To Do lists. He told us to concentrate on no more than three priorities at any one time. Humans are not bright enough to think about more than nine things at the same time—even those of us who claim to be brilliant at multi-tasking. And of that nine, we're unlikely to be able to successfully focus on more than three at a time. So, if your lists have too many level one tasks, or too many MUSTS, scheduled at the same time, you're not going to be able to be effective and you need to rethink either your objectives or your way of achieving them.

If you look back at my To Do list, you will notice there are far too many level one tasks on some days, particularly 15th. If I'd recorded my completion dates as well, you would see I finished a number of those tasks ahead of time, so in reality the load was spread more evenly across the days.

20.5 Urgency versus Importance

Even with the detailed To Do list which rules what I do each month, there are times when the number of items to be completed can become overwhelming. That's when I turn to the **Urgency versus Importance matrix**.

All tasks can be categorised in terms of their degree of urgency and their level of importance to the individual. Something is Urgent if it needs to be done now; something is Important if it contributes to a long-term goal. The two are not necessarily synonymous. Once tasks have been categorised, the strategy for deciding in which order to do them is relatively easy to determine.

Urgent and Important: For example, a call comes in from an editor looking for an article NOW to fill a hole that's just appeared in this week's paper. It's a paper that pays well and could provide you with lots more commissions in the future. **Strategy: drop everything and do it now.**

Non-Urgent and Important: For example, the corrections for your latest manuscript arrive with a request from the publisher to complete and return them within two weeks. A conservative estimate shows there is two days' work required. **Strategy: schedule it for later on.**

Urgent and Unimportant: For example, a close friend or relative you don't wish to offend makes a habit of phoning during the mornings 'for a chat' even though this is your prime writing time. **Strategy: Delegate it (in this case by use of an answering machine).**

Non-Urgent and Unimportant: A new game is doing the rounds on Facebook and a number of writing buddies are sending invitations to compete with them/feed their cows/send them gifts. **Strategy: Don't do it (block the requests without blocking the friends).**

You can see a representation of the Urgency versus Importance matrix on page 237 and there is a worked example at the end of this chapter.

This tool is variously attributed to Stephen Covey and to Dwight D Eisenhower. Covey certainly formalises the tool in his book *The 7 Habits of Highly Effective People* but it is predated by the well-known quote from

Eisenhower: "What is important is seldom urgent and what is urgent is seldom important."

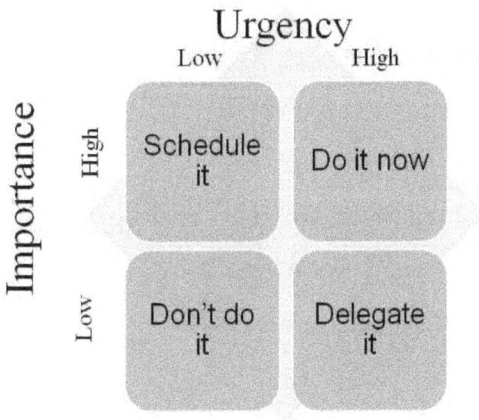

Urgency

	Low	High
High (Importance)	Schedule it	Do it now
Low (Importance)	Don't do it	Delegate it

Figure 20 Urgency versus Importance Matrix

There are a number of formal methods for employing this tool, including templates and apps. Personally, I just use the spreadsheet on which my To Do list is prepared.

20.6 Productivity Software

If you want something a little more specialised than spreadsheets and mind maps, there are all sorts of productivity software packages which can help you manage your projects and deadlines. Some are internet-based, while others work on all platforms, as well as most devices (such as the desktop, laptop, tablet or smartphone) but will sync across all devices via the internet. Simon Whaley, in Writing Magazine, recommends Todoist; and Remember The Milk. Steve Male of Chudleigh Writers' Circle and Swanwick Writers' Summer School recommends Toodledo. All of these have basic versions which are free to download and use.

20.7 Your Exercise: Time To Be Honest

You may think all the things getting in the way of your writing are justified, but if you look closely, there are probably lots of things you could do to free up more time. It's not lack of time that's the problem; it's lack of priorities. Try this exercise:

- Keep an activity diary over the course of a few days or a week. Don't spend too much time on it (that would be counter-productive) but jot down all the types of things you do, with a rough measure of the time taken (to the nearest hour or half-hour should be accurate enough). When I do this, I prepare a grid split into half-hour slots and then record what I'm doing at the start of each block of time. It's rough, but it's good enough for this purpose.

- Add up the time spent on similar activities; for example, writing press releases, pitching to event organisers and writing **promotional** tweets could all be recorded as marketing activities;

- Draw up a summary of the week in order of time spent, with the highest at the top;

- Use the urgency versus importance tool to categorise each activity;

- Starting at the top of the list, review honestly whether the time spent on each activity is justified in terms of benefit to your business, or whether it could be reduced or eliminated.

20.8 Conclusion

Whether you are a full-time writer, or whether you're fitting your writing around a full-time day job, it's more than likely you will find yourself with insufficient time to do everything you need and/or want to do. Time management is the key to being effective in this area. There are a variety of tools and techniques you can use to help prioritise your activities, including diaries, to do lists and apps or software.

20.9 Worked Example

On page 241, you can see an example of using the Urgency versus Importance matrix to determine priorities for a crowded ToDo list.

To Do	Urgency	Importance	Strategy
Short story competition with closing date in two days' time	H	H	Do this before anything else today
Short story competition with closing date at the end of next month	L	H	Schedule for three weeks' time
Publicity to be planned for a Literary Festival you are organising	H	H	Do this after your writing has been done
Publicity for the Literary Festival to be carried out	H	L	Delegate someone else on the committee to do it
Press release to be written for an ebook you are bringing out in six months' time	L	H	Check copy deadlines for intended target magazines and newspapers, then schedule one week before these.
Weekly blog posts for your own website	H	L	Use interviews and guest posts to reduce your own writing time. Plan posts in advance and draft some whenever you have spare time
Requests from friends on Facebook to take part in a weekly 'Like Swap'	L	L	Ignore requests
Monthly accounts to be brought up to date	L	H	Schedule half a day at the end of each month; record all transactions in a notebook as they occur, thus reducing time required to do the accounts
Guest posts to be written for blog tour associated with your book launch	L	H	Agree tour schedule with organiser or individual bloggers. Schedule writing time two weeks ahead of time
Weekly blog posts for your writing group's website which you are responsible for updating	H	L	Delegate writing to other members of the group (rotating to reduce their load); train someone else to do the technical aspects
Monthly newsletter for your distribution list, due to be sent out next week	L	H	Schedule for day before due date

Figure 21 U vs. I Analysis of To Do List

241

21. Problem Solving

21.1 Introduction

From time to time, no matter how well organised you are, you will have to deal with problems in your business. There are a whole range of tools and techniques available to help you identify, analyse and solve those problems. In this book, we're only going to look at some of the simplest ones, like brainstorming and Force Field Analysis and they are all qualitative. There are other, more complex ones, often quantitative, like histograms, scatter diagrams and process capability, but they're unlikely to be useful in your writing business, so we'll leave them to the statisticians and other problem-solving specialists.

If a problem-solving activity is centred on a symptom, it's likely the wrong problem will be 'solved'. That is why identification and definition of the problem is so important. This stage often takes longer than expected. In fact, if it's done properly, it may well be the longest part of the whole process. After all, once you know what the real problem is, the options for solving it are often relatively few and self-evident.

This book is about business processes rather than the art of writing. But it's possible to apply problem-solving techniques to the content of your work, as well as to the way you run your business. For example, in workshops at Swanwick Writers' Summer School, we've successfully applied some of these tools to novel plotting problems.

21.2 Mind Mapping

Mind mapping is a technique invented by Tony Buzan and is one of the most powerful tools in the box. A mind map is a graphic representation of an idea, an event or anything else you might want to think about. It uses all the cortical skills of your brain, including words, images, colours, and spatial awareness. It's based on the fact that your thought processes are not linear; mind mapping helps to make sense of a jumble of information.

Mind maps can be plain and functional—and for someone like me with little or no drawing skills, that's the way they tend to turn out. Or they can be colourful and creative. Check out Tony Buzan's website or his books for some beautiful examples. They tend to be highly coloured, containing lots of information, and will be personal to the designer. When I was studying for my MBA, I was able to construct a one-page mind map for each of my modules and this was a very effective revision method. But to anyone else, even someone taking the same course as me, they would probably be meaningless.

Mind maps can be drawn by hand in fact, Buzan's tool list for constructing one is very simple: blank paper; coloured pens and pencils; your brain; and your imagination. However, they can also be drawn on the computer. There are free software packages available, but for more functionality, it's worth investing in a proprietary package. I currently use Mind Manager for all my project planning. However, I've just been introduced to Scapple from Literature & Latte, the folk behind Scrivener (which we're going to talk about in chapter 22). I've not used it yet, but it comes highly recommended and checking it out is on my To Do list for next month.

You can see an example of a hand-drawn mind map, generated as part of the planning process for Chudleigh Literary Festival, on page 247. For examples of computer-generated mind maps, refer back to pages 213 and 230.

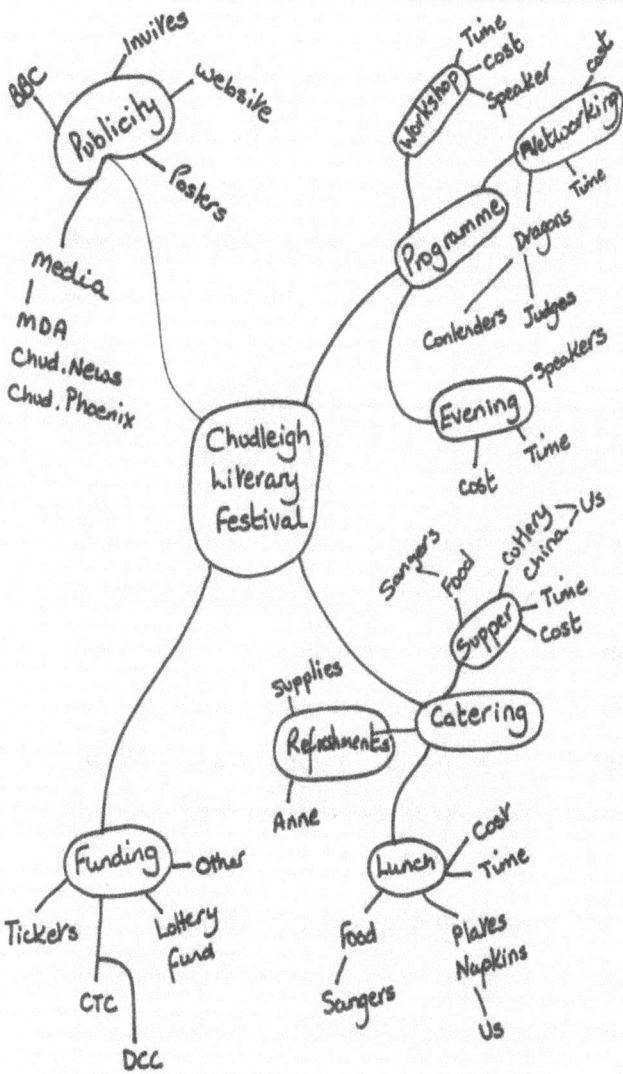

Figure 22 Hand-drawn Mind Map

21.3 Brainstorming

Brainstorming is a means by which collective experience is brought into the problem-solving process and is a way of generating large numbers of ideas rapidly. It works best when done by a group of people rather than an individual, since several people working together, and thinking laterally, are likely to come up with more ideas as a group than the total gained by adding their individual lists together.

Suppose someone is asked to list all the possible uses for a paper cup as a new business venture (a common warm-up exercise for brainstorming). They might come up with five suggestions quite quickly or even ten. After that, most people find it a struggle. On the other hand, if everyone is shouting out their ideas and they're being recorded on a flip-chart, one person's off-the-wall suggestion might trigger other ideas from members of the group. For example, the suggestion 'false nose' might lead to other suggestions such as 'part of a mask', 'part of a collage' or 'hat for a doll'.

Brainstorming requires a facilitator who writes the question on the flip-chart, records all the answers from the group and makes sure the rules of brainstorming, as shown below, are followed. Members of the group either take it in turns to make a suggestion or just shout them out as they think of them. The latter approach is more spontaneous but harder for the facilitator to record.

Rules of brainstorming

- There should be no criticism or evaluation;

- Freewheeling is encouraged (and as a writer, the ability to use your creativity to come up with innovative ideas is something you should be good at);

- Concentrate on getting the maximum number of ideas;

- Record every idea, even repetition;

- Incubate all the ideas; do not reject anything out of hand.

Application

So, how can brainstorming be useful? We tend to work as individuals much of the time. But most of us are part of a team at least occasionally. There's the support team made up of your family plus anyone who provides services to you in your business: book-keeper, accountant, agent, editor, cover designers, printers and so on. Or there's your customer base; or your writing groups. Depending on what problem you're trying to solve, a quick brainstorming session with some of these groups might be very helpful.

For example, you have a new project offered to you. You already have a packed diary for the next three months, with commitments you can't break. But this is a great opportunity and one you don't want to pass up. Sitting alone at your desk, you might feel overwhelmed with the difficulty of getting everything done on schedule. But sit down with some of the support team to bounce a few ideas around and who knows what solutions might offer themselves. Perhaps one of the kids might come up with a brilliant suggestion for how to reduce your workload in one area, freeing up time for the new project.

As another example, you know that moment when you're struggling with the plot of your latest novel or short story; where one of the main characters just won't do what you want them to? Well, a brainstorming session with a group of other writers is often a great way of working through the problem and coming up with all sorts of solutions. Some of them will be off-the-wall and inappropriate; but one or two are likely to be good solid ideas that you can use to get the story back on track. I've used this technique very successfully on a number of occasions with Exeter Writers, one of the groups to which I belong.

21.4 Fish-Bone Diagram

This technique has several names in common usage. It was originally called the Ishikawa Diagram after Dr Karou Ishikawa, who developed it in the 1960s. It's also called the Cause and Effect Diagram since it is used to organise and structure possible causes for a given effect (or problem). Its most popular name comes from the shape it takes on construction—that of a fish skeleton. The steps in construction of a Fish-Bone diagram are shown below.

Steps In Construction

- Write the effect or problem being investigated in a box on the right-hand side of the flip-chart;

- Draw a horizontal line from the centre of the box across the paper;

- Add side branches or ribs;

- Identify suitable categories (sub-groups) of causes and label side branches;

- List the possible causes on the sheet under the appropriate category.

The Fish-Bone diagram is a more structured form of idea generation than brainstorming, since it identifies a number of categories or sub-groups under which the various ideas are listed. These are often standard sets such as the five elements that go to make up all processes: *(wo)man, machine, method, material* and *environment,* although they can be completely new groupings if more appropriate. I tend to think of this technique as a combination of mind mapping and brainstorming.

Example

Let's imagine you've self-published your first book. You've had a launch party, sold a respectable number of copies—whatever that means—but after a few weeks, sales have dried up. You decide to take a critical look at your marketing strategy, using the 4Ps: product, place, price and promotion.

- **Product:** it could be you need to do some more work on proofreading or editing; maybe the cover design needs tweaking; or you might consider changing the title.

- **Place**: perhaps you aren't selling in the places your typical reader tends to buy books. If you've written a cosy romance, with the older reader in mind, or a history of how your village coped during WWI, then a print book for sale in the local post office for example might be more appropriate than an ebook or a Print On Demand book, only available online.

- **Price**: is your book on offer at too high a price? Or is it too cheap? How does it compare with your main competitors in the marketplace?

- **Promotion**: are you spending all your promotional time on Twitter saying, "buy my book, buy my book"? Are you ignoring potential readers who want to make contact via email?

You can see the start of this analysis, using the Fish-Bone diagram, on page 255. There are lots of other possible causes you could consider, and you might think of different categories that are more appropriate than the 4Ps.

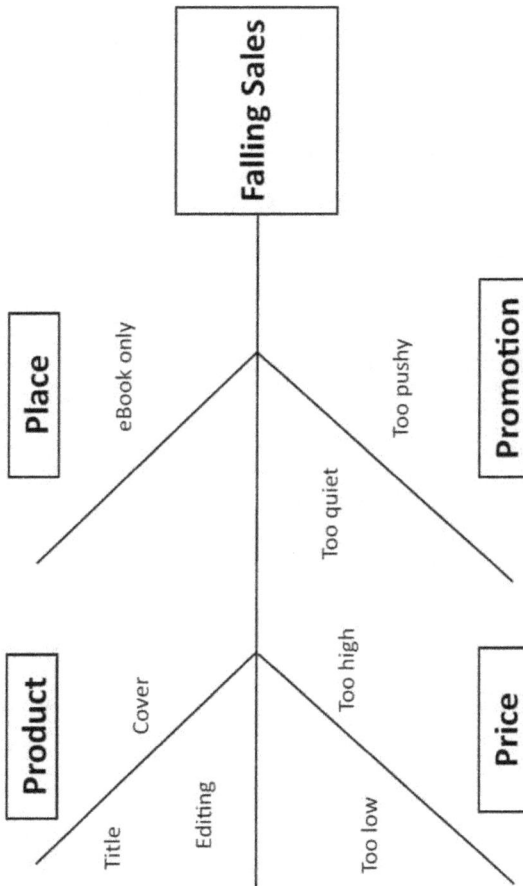

Figure 23 Fish Bone Diagram

21.5 Force Field Analysis

Reducing or eliminating a problem will often require an element of change. For any change, there will be a series of forces driving it forward and another series of forces restraining it. These will include forces relating to money, time and especially people. While some people positively welcome change, for others it can be a time of threat or fear.

The examination of these forces was developed by Kurt Lewin into Force Field Analysis (1997), which can be used in two ways:

- to decide whether a proposed change is possible and feasible;

- and to decide how to facilitate the change in the most effective way.

Steps In Setting Up a Force Field Analysis

- Ensure the proposed change is clearly defined and understood by everyone in the same way;

- Draw a vertical line down the centre of a flip-chart sheet;

- List the positive, driving forces on the left-hand side of the sheet, with arrows pointing towards the right;

- List the negative, restraining forces on the right-hand side of the sheet, with arrows pointing to the left;

- Score all forces between 1(weak) and 5 (strong); I know I said earlier that we were just going to talk about qualitative techniques, but this is only pseudo-quantitative, since the scoring of strength is an assessment, based on your opinion and experience, rather than a true measurement;

- On the diagram, the line in the centre represents the status quo and the extreme right-hand side represents the required situation;

- To determine feasibility, scores are summed for the drivers and for the restrainers. A feasible change is one where the former score is higher than the latter one.

Different lengths of arrow can be used to represent different strengths of force. In order to move from the status quo to the required position, it is necessary either to strengthen the driving forces or (more often) weaken the restraining forces.

In practice, any action to strengthen a driving force will tend to result in the opposing restraining forces becoming stronger too. **The best way to move towards the ideal situation is to work on weakening the restraining forces.**

Worked Example

Let's assume you work in the editorial department of a local newspaper but would really like to give up the 'day job' and become a full-time writer. Let's use Force Field Analysis to analyse the situation. Is it feasible and how can you bring about your dream?

When you consider the positive forces, those driving you towards making the change, and their relative strengths, you conclude:

- you lack job satisfaction (4);

- you have a passion for writing (5);

- you have had some success with short story competitions (3);

- and your family is relatively supportive of the idea (4).

On the other hand:

- you have a high monthly mortgage payment to service (5);

- you are scared you might not be good enough (3);

- you know the competition out there is high (3);

- and you don't want to let your boss down (4).

If you sum the two sets of scores, you get a positive score of 16 and a negative one of 15. So, the proposed change is feasible—but only just. And remember the scores are only based on your opinion, rather than on solid fact.

In order to facilitate the change, you need to reduce the restraints where possible. You can work on your fear of failure. You can't do much about the competition, apart from making sure your work is the best it possibly can be. Your loyalty to your boss is a fact of life, although it might be alleviated by providing practical solutions for how she might plug the gap when you leave. But the most tangible force, the one you can tackle practically, is the mortgage. As so often, it may all come down to money. You can see this example of Force Field Analysis on page 261.

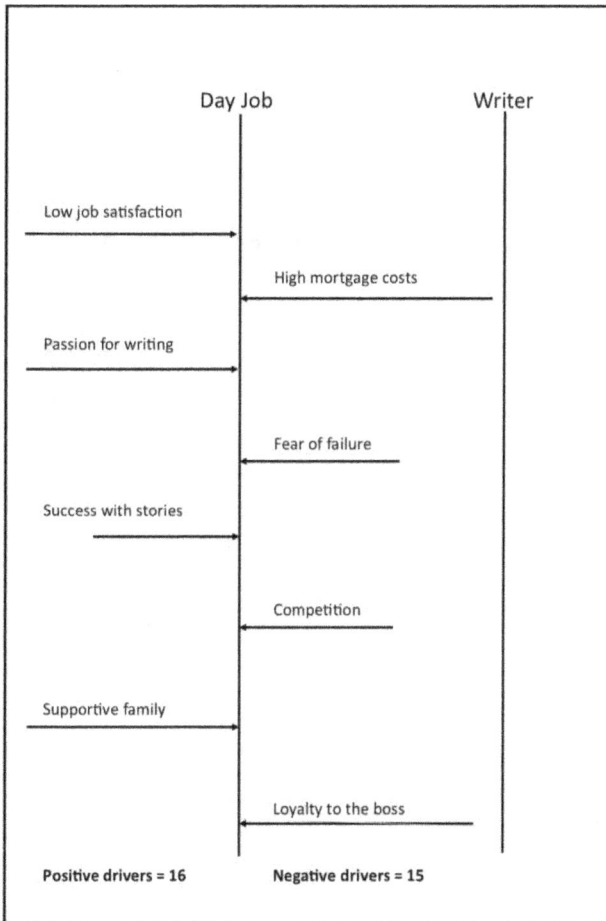

Figure 24 Force Field Analysis

21.6 Conclusion

We all face problems from time to time. Being able to analyse those problems and identify the causes is a major step towards finding an appropriate solution. There are several types of problem-solving tools, some of which are presented in this chapter. They can be used simply and easily, often with no more than a set of coloured pens and a notebook or flip-chart.

22. Miscellany

22.1 Introduction

To finish this book, we're going to look at a few other ways of improving your productivity and getting the job done better. They don't fit into a neat category—and this is by no means a definitive list. These are just some of the tools and techniques I've gathered along the way which help me work more effectively.

22.2 Timers

Even with all your plans, diaries and productivity measures, there will be times when you think: "I've got nothing to write about!" or "Nothing I write makes any sense" or even "I can't be bothered!" When you get to that point, the temptation is to take the afternoon off, go for a walk, curl up with a book—or head for Facebook instead. And sometimes that's a good thing to do. No-one can work continuously, and you need to give your mind time to rest. Everyone deserves the occasional 'duvet day'. But you need to remember you are not just a writer, but also a business owner and this is your job, so not writing is generally not an option.

When I get to this stage, I find the so-called Pomodoro technique very effective. Invented in the 1980s by Francesco Cirillo, it's based on a work pattern of short bursts (traditionally twenty-five minutes) interspersed with breaks of three to five minutes' duration. Even if the idea of a day or half a day at the keyboard is difficult, most people will be able to concentrate for twenty-five minutes at a time. I generally find after a couple of sessions, I'm so involved in the writing, I forget to set the timer—or I keep writing even after the timer has gone off.

22.3 Open Source Software

There is the occasional business which, even today, works without using a computer. But writers do not come into that category. Some of us may produce our initial drafts by hand, but our customers will expect us to deliver the final product electronically or at least typed. The basic software packages you need will therefore include word processing and spreadsheets.

For most people, this will mean Microsoft Office or its little sister, Microsoft Works, although this is now a discontinued program. But if you don't want to make the investment in those, there are some free, safe options available: check out the Apache Open Office or LibreOffice suite of products. I use the latter and the documents produced are compatible with equivalent Office products.

A word of warning: there are all sorts of offers for free software downloads on the internet. Some of them, like these two, are safe, reputable products. But others are not, so it's important to always do some research before downloading anything to your computers.

22.4 Spreadsheets

I've mentioned these several times already, and it's fair to say I find them an invaluable tool. I use spreadsheets for my To Do lists, for my project plans, and for my marketing schedules. On the basis that pictures are quicker and easier to assimilate than words, I use colour coding to record progress. I mainly use the traffic-light system: red for overdue; yellow for in progress; and green for complete.

22.5 Scrivener

There are several different software packages available for writers. The one I use is Scrivener which is great for organising long pieces of work, like novels or textbooks. In fact, I use it for short stories as well, breaking each one into a series of scenes I can manipulate separately. It allows the order of chapters or scenes to be changed very easily. There is also space for linking all the research and ancillary files together in one place. It may look complicated at first sight, but there's a detailed tutorial worth working through before beginning a live project. It's not a free package, but the one-off cost of $45 for either the Windows or Mac version, was an investment that certainly paid off for me in time-saving. And there's a great 30-day free trial, which lasts for as long as it takes you to use it on 30 separate days. The package was referred to me by a fellow Devonian writer, Michael Jecks, who estimates it saves him 4 months per year.

22.6 Globalised Links

Anyone who has a book on the Amazon platform will know what a hassle it can be to provide links for the different national websites in your promotional material. The more effective option is to provide a globalised link that will take any user to their 'home' site.

There are a variety of options available for this. I use Genius Link, which provides a link that works across countries, devices and stores. It has more functionality that that—and one of these days, I will get around to investigating things like Associates Programs—but as a method of providing a single link that works for all potential purchasers, it's a great time-saver. I'm indebted to fellow Swanwicker, Sally Jenkins, for telling me about it.

22.7 Limit Your Experts

When you're planning to do something—like start up and run your own small writing business—a big problem you face these days is information overload. There are not only books, like this one, offering advice, but also YouTube videos, podcasts, radio and TV programmes, and the ubiquitous free webinar.

Now I'm a real sucker for a bargain and will quite often sign on these webinars, especially if it's on a topic where my skills need updating. But the trouble is, there are just so many of them. And they'll either all tell you the same thing or—even worse—give you completely conflicting advice. Because this industry of ours is in a state of flux and no-one has all the answers. And what works for one person doesn't necessarily work for everyone else.

And by signing up, you're on yet another person's mailing list, receiving all their marketing material from now on. Of course, I'm not saying mailing lists and marketing material are bad things; quite the contrary. But an inbox clogged up with dozens of emails that you don't have time to open is just counter-productive for you and a waste of time and money for the sender.

I would suggest you try out a few experts, decide which ones suit your approach best, and stick with them. I'm a member of the Alliance of Independent Authors (ALLi), and most of my advice comes from them, especially when they put on their online self-publishing conferences two or three times a year. I read everything Joanna Penn writes on marketing; follow Mark Dawson's Self-Publishing Formula for some great podcasts and training modules; take my creativity tips from Orna Ross; and am an active member of PR School with Natalie Trice. And that's it. Otherwise I'd spend more time learning than I do writing and marketing my own work.

Of course, I'm not necessarily suggesting you use the same experts as me; although a word-of-mouth recommendation is always important. But I am suggesting you avoid becoming overwhelmed by deciding how many you can work with effectively and ignoring the rest.

22.8 Conclusion

Productivity is all about finding out what works for you. In this final chapter, we've looked at a variety of tools and techniques that work for me. Try them out and see how you get on. If they aren't useful, abandon them and try something else. After all, it's your business; you are the only person who can decide what works best for you.

Enjoyed This Book?

Reviews and recommendations are very important to an author and help contribute to a book's success. If you have enjoyed *The Business of Writing* please recommend it to your writer friends and colleagues or, better still, buy them a copy for their birthday or Christmas. And please consider posting a review on your preferred review site.

About Elizabeth Ducie

Elizabeth Ducie has an MBA (Masters in Business Administration) from the School of Management at Cranfield University, under her married name of McCormick, and a wealth of experience in different types of businesses. For more than twenty years, she ran a technical consultancy, a limited company which she set up and co-owned with her husband, Michael. For part of that time, she was also employed by a large multi-national corporation. She has worked with a wide range of businesses and other organisations across the world. She is now self-employed as a full-time author and publisher.

Elizabeth is an experienced trainer and presenter who has been writing training manuals and courses throughout her career. Her workshops on *The Business of Writing* are a regular feature at the annual Writers' Summer School in Swanwick, Derbyshire.

Elizabeth has written throughout her life. She was initially published at the age of fourteen, when she won a competition in the local newspaper. Her technical writing runs to millions of words in reports, manuals and courses, plus articles for scientific journals and several text books. These days she concentrates on fiction and creative non-fiction. In addition to *The Business of Writing*, she has published three collections of short stories and three novels..

Other Books by Elizabeth Ducie

Business Books

The Business of Writing: Part 1 Business Start-Up *

The Business of Writing: Part 2 Finance Matters *

The Business of Writing: Part 3 Improving Effectiveness *

The Business of Writing: Part 4 Independent Publishing *

The Business of Writing: Part 5 Workbook

* ebook only

Novels

Corruption!

Deception!

Counterfeit!

Gorgito's Ice Rink

Miscellaneous

Sunshine and Sausages

Parcels in the Rain and Other Writing

Written with Sharon Cook

Life is Not a Trifling Affair

Life is Not a Bed of Roses

To contact Elizabeth or to find out more about

Chudleigh Phoenix Publications:

elizabeth@elizabethducie.co.uk;

www.elizabethducie.co.uk;